"TRUST"

I KNOW...

POPS

WRITTEN BY: "FOREVER GRATEFUL..."

Table of Contents

About the Author   v

Introduction   6

Chapter 1: The Blackfoot   8

Chapter 2: Family Merger   12

Chapter 3: The Chinese Wall   16

Chapter 4: Benchmark to Indian Flats   23

Chapter 5: Indian Flats Campsite   35

Chapter 6: Table Rock   46

Chapter 7: The Fall   53

Chapter 8: "Midnight Ride"   63

Chapter 9: Tasks to Complete   69

Chapter 10: "*trUst*"   74

Chapter 11: The Rescue   85

Chapter 12: The Postcard   94

Chapter 13: shared with you...   97

ABOUT THE AUTHOR

The author **"Forever Grateful"** lived the *UNIMAGINABLE* event you are about to read about. Which real-life character in this story is the author? Going to leave that up to you, the reader, to decide.

"Forever Grateful" for the fact that human beings can pull together and focus on *"What's Right"* rather than *"Who's Right?"*

I work in a profession where eleven team members doing *"What's Right"* leads to EXTREME EXECUTION. Every member's one-eleventh is crucial to obtain the *"earned"* eleven-elevenths needed to dominate an opponent inside the rectangle. Needless to say, *"Who's Right,"* in my profession, is irrelevant to the desired outcome, **regardless** of what our cell phones tell us after the contest.

Every reader of this book was born with an **ACE** in their hand at birth. I encourage you to *"double down"* on that **ACE** every chance you get when tough times creep into life. Embrace U, trUst U, and be DECISIVE on what horse you pick out of that corral to saddle each morning. *"**Spurs**"* will be needed at times to get the one-eleventh your life teammates need - #selfstrengthisundefeated!

Never forget the words *"y**OURS**"* and *"**OURS**"* share four letters for a reason ... **"Give feels so much better than Get..."**

INTRODUCTION

I received a Christmas gift from my twenty-three-year-old daughter that inspired me to author this book. The gift was a leather-bound notebook, and she left me this note of inspiration on the first page:

> Daddio,
>
> I remember when I was little begging you over and over to tell me a story. I would hang on to every word as you re-counted how your siblings would terrorize you...about you and Bart getting into trouble...stories Grandpa Fry and Grandpa McMahon passed down to you, and all the lessons you learned along the way.
>
> I loved those stories. Not only were they entertaining, but because they showed me more about the man I thought hung the moon. A man who was kind, a little stubborn, hardworking, and full of love. Your gift of wisdom proves a life lived in full.
>
> I wanted to give you this notebook with the hope that you would use it to tell your own story. So that one day I can continue to learn from you in these pages, and I can

---

Never been able to tell that child no, so here we go…

This is a **TRUE** story passed down to me that is set in the *"remote"* Bob Marshall Wilderness Complex of Montana in 1973. When I say **"remote,"** I mean **ZERO** means of communication available!

All readers must **"understand"** that there was no internet, no cell phone, no TikTok, no Snapchat, and no email in the United States in 1973. Think of The Bob Marshall Wilderness Complex as modern-day ***"OFF THE GRID ON STEROIDS."***

To all of you who choose to move forward through the pages of this book, I suggest you:

"Strap on your spurs, keep your head back, and get ready for one hell of a ride!"

CHAPTER 1:
THE BLACKFOOT

Jack McMahon dropped into **the *Blackfoot River*** between Avon and Garrison, Montana, that late spring evening in 1967, expecting to land his fill of Native Western Slope Cutthroat Trout before nightfall.

On his many travels from Helena to Missoula, he had stopped his car to watch fly fishermen pull trout out of the exact hole he was about to cast into. Cast after cast, he watched that hopper move along the current "***untouched***" as cutthroat rose and fed all around him.

Downriver Dick Fryhover was in his usual evening "groove" catching "cuts" left and right with each cast of his Fenwick rod. He could not help but "***notice***" the struggle going on 150 yards up the river from him. Fry was a "legend" on these waters, and within an hour, he decided to walk up the railroad tracks that lined the river to offer a word of advice to the Blackfoot Greenhorn.

"Howdy partner, how's the fishing?" Fry questioned as he reached the edge of the water Jack was standing in.

"Can't get them even to sniff this hopper," Jack responded hopelessly.

"Little early in the season for the hopper, my friend. I got just what you need right here in my fly box if you'd like to throw one on," Fry offered.

"I would really appreciate anything you've got to offer. First time fly fishing - getting my tail kicked in as you can undoubtedly see," Jack replied, defeated.

"Name's Dick Fryhover. I run Brown's Sporting Goods there in Helena," Fry said as he reached out to Jack's outstretched hand.

"Jack McMahon. I'm a surgeon and reside in Helena also. Great to meet you, Dick." Jack replied, shaking Dick's hand.

"Let's throw on a Royal Wulff – the "cuts" love them. This fly matches the pattern you see the risers feeding on in the water this evening," Fry responded while reaching into his fly box for one.

Dick Fryhover took the next half an hour giving Jack a **"*world-class*"** personal tutorial on the **"*art*"** of fly fishing the banks, ripples, and deep, slow water of The Blackfoot River. No stone was left unturned with Fry ... How to tie a fly on properly? How to cast properly? How to "*read*" the water to identify where the fish were feeding?

Jack McMahon had *"literally"* just fallen into a once-in-a-lifetime learning experience that, unbeknownst to him, would propel the two men into a RARE lifelong friendship few men are blessed to share.

"Your turn, Jack," Fry said, handing the rod back to Jack after stripping in his fourth cutthroat in a row.

"Cast it right on the edge of that foam line running along the fast water, Jack. Keep mending that line to keep it above the drift level of the Wulff. As soon as that fly drifts down that slope, hitting the slow water, be ready," Fry instructed.

Jack sent a "smooth", deliberate cast upstream exactly as instructed to the edge of the fast water, keeping a hopeful eye on the Royal Wulff as it made its way downstream to the edge of the hole.

"**BANG!**" That cutty hit the Wulff just like Fry said it would as it drifted into the slow water. Jack McMahon had his first Montana cutthroat trout tugging on his line.

"Keep the line tight and that rod up in the direction of the bank, Jack. No need to try and get him on the reel," Fry instructed as Jack slowly stripped the trout in.

As Jack fought and stripped the cut to within two feet of where he was standing, Dick reached down with his net and scooped the trout out of the Blackfoot.

"That was incredible, amazing what a little guidance can do in life. Beyond grateful to you, Dick," Jack exclaimed with a big smile as he released the trout back into the water.

The two men spent the next hour and a half fishing and conversing a quarter mile of The Blackfoot downstream. Fry patiently shot advice to his new friend as both men pulled in their fair share of trout using that *"Wulff pattern"* until darkness set in.

As both men reached their cars, Jack and Dick exchanged phone numbers and made plans to get their two families together soon. Little did they know ***"their <u>word</u> of truth and trUst would formulate into a lifelong bond"*** stemming from this chance encounter on the Blackfoot River.

CHAPTER 2:
FAMILY MERGER

Left to Right: *Jack McMahon, Joanie McMahon, Marge Fryhover, Dick Fryhover, and Mike McMahon sharing a meal at one of the many campsites they shared along the banks of the Smith River. (1977 family photo).*

Dick Fryhover and Jack McMahon kept their "<u>word</u>" on getting their respective families together. In fact, through the years, the families were together so much that their bond could be considered "inseparable."

Dick and Marge Fryhover met and married after Dick returned home from serving his country in the Korean War. The couple eventually settled down in Helena, Montana, to raise their family consisting of three daughters: Denise, Darla, and Deah. Mr. Fry also had a son, Dick Jr., from a previous marriage, who lived in Colorado with his mother.

Jack and Joanie McMahon met and got married while both were attending Saint Louis University. Upon finishing Jack's medical residency in St. Louis, the McMahons chose Helena, Montana, to raise their family and begin Jack's surgical practice. The McMahon's had 6 daughters and 9 sons: Kathy, Charlie Mott, Jack Jr., Stevie, Ron Mott (aka Rosie), Joan Marie (aka Missy), Joe (aka Pat), Nancy Mott, Mary Anne (aka Toots), Mike, Sunny Mott, Tim, Mary Ellen (aka Oly), Tom (aka Tommy), and Dick whom was named after Dick Fryhover. Jack and Joanie lost their son Stevie to an accident in the fall of 1966. Kathy was taken into foster care in 1969 and eventually fully adopted by Jack and Joanie. Charlie Mott, Ron Mott, Nancy Mott, and Sunny Mott were taken into foster care by Jack and Joanie in 1975 and have remained part of the two families ever since.

Marge Fryhover and Joanie McMahon were the true "architects" of this "lifelong merger" of families. Unwavering selflessness and decisive embrace rained down twenty-four hours a day from their hearts to their children and spouses. Camping, float trips, sledding, popcorn cakes, treasure hunts on birthdays spent in the backcountry, Mrs. Fry's famous chili, and endless nights spent around a campfire enjoying stories are just a few joyous memories shared by all through the formative years of raising the two families.

Around 1972, Dick and Jack's love of the outdoors drove them to form "Backcountry Outfitters." An "outfitter" provides the necessary gear, equipment, logistics, and, in the case of this company, the "**guided**" services for hunting and fishing expeditions into Montana's backcountry.

Dick and Jack rotated between the Smith River drainage near White Sulphur Springs, Montana and the South Fork of the Flathead River in the Bob Marshall Wilderness Area to guide fishing trips in the summer months during the 1970's. The guided fishing trips into the South Fork required two days of travel by horseback to reach the river. Fry and Jack used the Benchmark Trailhead, twenty-nine miles west of Augusta, Montana, as an entry point into this Bob Marshall Wilderness Area due to the vast number of stock corrals the forest service provided there.

In the fall through the end of November, they provided guided hunting trips by horseback into the remote Helena National Forest area outside of Lincoln, Montana. The Indian Meadows Trailhead up Copper Creek Road, and in later years, the "secret" Fickler Ranch Trailhead up Alice Creek Road, were used as entry points into this Wilderness area by Fry and Jack. Caribou, Fickler, Baking Powder, Falls Creek, Elk, and Silver King Ridges provided a great deal of elk and deer harvest for the company's customers in the 1970's.

In 1971, shortly after the inception of the outfitting business, Jack and Joanie McMahon purchased a one-hundred-twenty-acre parcel up Alice Creek Road near Lincoln, Montana. This remote property was located about fifty-five miles northeast of Helena. Fry and Jack used this property as a ***base of operations*** to pasture the horses, mules, store their tack, river rafts, and supplies. The Great Falls and Helena airports served as transportation hubs for the out-of-state customers who were transported by vehicle to the Smith River, or Benchmark and Indian Meadows Trailheads.

Dick Fryhover oversaw a majority of the *"operations and logistics"* of the outfitting business. Jack McMahon's surgical practice required a great deal of attention, yet every free minute he had was spent helping Fry from June through November. The guides, cooks, and wranglers they hired into the business were one heck of a *"unique"* cast of characters, creating lasting memories for all! Griff Davidson, Jimmy Hake, Don Carter, and Tim Gleason will always be *"cherished"* as lifelong family members of the Fryhover's and McMahon's.

CHAPTER 3:
THE CHINESE WALL

The summer of 1973 fishing season was coming to a close for Backcountry Outfitters on the South Fork of the Flathead by mid-August. Dr. Jack McMahon decided to finish the summer off with a backcountry vacation into the Chinese Wall area of the Bob Marshall Wilderness, consisting of family and a close friend's family, before the children headed back to school.

That close friend was Dr. C. Rollins "Rollo" Hanlon, his wife Dr. Margaret "Peg" Hanlon, and three of their daughters, Mary (14), Martha (12), and Sarah (10). From 1969 – 1986, "Rollo", as his peers affectionately called him, served as the Executive Director of the American College of Surgeons. Dr. Hanlon performed the first open heart surgery in St. Louis in 1956, followed by a series of other firsts, including the first prosthetic valve (1962), pacemaker (1966), and coronary bypass (1969). Dr. Hanlon was the department chair at Saint Louis University while Jack McMahon was a medical student at SLU from 1952 - 1955. Jack McMahon regarded Dr. Hanlon as his lifelong "***career mentor.***"

The early morning of August 14, 1973, had Joanie McMahon feeling a dual sense of excitement and nervous anxiety as the vehicles made their way west up the bumpy dirt road between Augusta and the trailhead at Benchmark.

Joanie had looked forward to this backcountry vacation for months, yet two hours earlier, she had left her two-year-old son Dick in the care of her twenty-year-old daughter Kathy.

"They'll be fine, love. Kathy's got him," Jack said, "*innately*" feeling Joanie's concern from the passenger seat of the pickup.

"I know," Joanie responded, smiling back at Jack, appreciating his deliberate concern of her "*maternal*" emotions.

"What are you looking forward to the most?" Jack asked, attempting to get his bride's mind onto something else.

"Seeing the kids' faces once we get up to view the Chinese Wall, I suppose," Joanie replied.

"I can't wait to see them pull rainbow and browns out of the Sun River at the Indian Flats campsite," Jack blurted back with immense pride as any true fly fisherman would.

"What's your plan for Oly and Tommy?" Joanie asked about their five-year-old blonde bundle of endless energy daughter and shy, polar-opposite four-year-old son.

"How about we throw them both on Lightning? That mare will look out for the two of them. Oly can manage the reins, and we will put Tommy in behind her on the saddle," Jack responded, referencing the eleven-year-old mare he trusted the most from the herd of trail horses they owned.

"I agree, but let's be sure they are behind Dick or yourself at all times on the trail," Joanie insisted as Jack nodded his head in agreement, slowly finishing the drive down the hill into the stock corral area at the Benchmark Trailhead.

Jack's eyes surveyed the stock tied to the corral posts, saddled and loaded with great internal appreciation of Dick Fryhover and the three young wranglers, Tim Gleason, son Jack Jr., and son Joe, all of whom had spent the previous night at the trailhead.

Dick Fryhover was grabbing his saddle bags out of his white Chevy Suburban, affectionately nicknamed "*Brophy*," when he saw the vehicles pulling in.

He hollered over to the boys, "See that red suburban pulling in at the edge of the corrals? That is Dr. Hanlon and his family from St. Louis. Head over there and properly introduce yourselves, if you would? Give them a hand getting that suburban unloaded. You will need to grab more **_manties_** and rope out of the front of the tack trailer. Once you finish "*mantie-ing up*" their gear, I will help you load it onto the remaining pack mules and pack horses, and we will shag ass up the trail."

"Roger that," they replied in unison as the three of them started towards the Hanlons' suburban.

<u>Note</u>: *"Manties"* are canvas tarps packers use to "*<u>wrap up and secure</u>*" gear, supplies, and hay to transport it on the pack saddles of their stock. *"Mantie-ing up"* is a slang term for the "*roped wrapping procedure*" used to secure the gear in the canvas tarp. (*See completed "white canvas gear manties" in the photo provided above*)

As the Hanlons stepped out of the red suburban, the three young wranglers were there as instructed, openly welcoming them.

"Dr. Hanlon and Mrs. Hanlon, I'm Tim Gleason. This here is Doc's sons Joe and Jack Jr. We were sent over to welcome you and give you a hand unloading your gear," Tim said, reaching out his hand to Dr. Hanlon.

"Greatly appreciate your courtesy, good men," Dr. Hanlon responded as he reached for Tim's hand.

"Let me introduce you to my wife, Dr. Peg Hanlon, and our three daughters, Mary, Martha, and Sarah."

"Three doctors on this trip, sure makes me feel secure," Tim Gleason said, recognizing how proudly Dr. Hanlon introduced his bride, Dr. Peg Hanlon. "Hope we won't need any of your expertise on this trip Doc."

"We are 100% on vacation," Peg exclaimed exuberantly, glancing lovingly at her three wide-eyed daughters exiting the vehicle. "The five of us have been looking forward to this trip for months! St. Louis, Missouri, does not look like this. That drive up from Augusta was beautiful."

"Wait until we get into that Sun River drainage, ma'am. Nothing prettier in the world than coming down that ridge on horseback, seeing those valley meadows open giving room for that river to flow through," Jack Jr. added.

As Jack, Fry, Tim Gleason (17), Jack Jr. (16), and Joe (13) finished the manties and loading up the remaining mules, the remaining McMahon children, Missy (14), Toots (9), Mike (8), Tim (7), Oly (5) and Tommy (4) took turns giving riding tutorials to the Hanlon girls and their parents aboard trail horses Lightning, Blaze, Malibu, and Joker.

The plan was to make camp about fifteen miles in along the West Fork of the Sun River at a spot Dick Fryhover called Indian Flats. They would use this campsite as a *"base camp."* Logistically, this location put them within a three-hour *"day ride"* of Table Rock, which would provide a magnificent view and picnic location below the Chinese Wall.

An hour and a half after pulling into the Benchmark Trailhead stock corrals, the McMahon and Hanlon families were on horseback, ready to begin their journey up Trail #202 to merge with Trail #203 into the West Fork of the Sun

River drainage. Dick Fryhover, Tim Gleason, Jack McMahon Jr., and Joe McMahon *"shagged ass"* out about forty-five minutes earlier with the pack string in hopes of beating them to Indian Flats to begin getting camp set up.

Note: *Yellow line marks the trail of this "Journey in the Bob" and all its main stops ... 1. Benchmark Trailhead, 2. Indian Flats Campsite, 3. Table Rock – Chinese Wall*

CHAPTER 4: BENCHMARK TO INDIAN FLATS

"There is a bridge about two hundred yards up the trail. It will swing a little bit as we cross it with the horses. Hold onto that saddle horn if you get feeling a little nervous." Jack Mahon Sr. alerted the riders before giving the stallion Romeo a kick to begin their journey, leaving Benchmark.

Sure enough, that swinging bridge began to "*dance*" as the stock made their way swiftly across it.

Dr. Hanlon glanced back to check on Mary, Martha, Sarah, and Peg as he neared the halfway point of the bridge crossing.

"You ok back there?" he hollered to the girls loudly over the echoing "*steel-shod*" hooves of the stock smashing down on the wooden bridge.

"All good, Dad," Sarah and Mary responded in unison, clenching down on their saddle horns aboard the steady mares Malibu and Diala.

"I think I'm going to get sick," daughter Martha said, giggling nervously as her insides turned circles aboard the painted gelding known as Joker.

Dr. Peg Hanlon said nothing back to her concerned husband. Her singular focus was on "*two-handing*" the saddle horn as instructed, along with "*squeezing*" her knees into the sides of the veteran mare Blaze she was riding. The silent "*trUst*" she bestowed upon Blaze as that bridge "*see-sawed*" above the South Fork of the Sun River would never be felt again in her lifetime.

Jack McMahon got to the top of the rise above the bridge, turning around in his saddle, he glanced down the entire column of riders to his fourteen-year-old daughter Missy. Missy caught eye contact with her father and "*flashed*" him a big smile with a "*double thumbs up,*" reassuring him all was good. "*Mother Miss*" took immense pride in her assigned role as the last rider watching over her "*flock*" on many a family trail ride.

Three miles up the trail, the pack train was at a momentary standstill. One of the packs on Festus, a dark black mule, had slipped and needed fixing. As Tim Gleason adjusted the pack, Dick Fryhover sat on his trusted favorite gelding, Spider, giving no instruction. No need to waste words on the experienced seventeen-year-old *"boyfriend"* of his eldest daughter, Denise, who, unbeknownst to Fry at the time, would later become his future son-in-law.

"Got her Fry. Let's roll," Tim hollered as he climbed back on Charley.

Fry gave Spider a soft kick to his belly, and the massive young gelding *"propped his ears"* forward and began leading the pack string back up the trail.

Dick Fryhover, without hesitation, began to sing proudly, for all inhabitants of the Bob Marshall Wilderness to hear this world-famous 1971 Hit Single by the late great Charley Pride:

"Whenever I chance to meet ...

some old friends on the street ...

they wonder how does a man get to be this way.

I've always got a smiling face ...

any time and any place …

and every time they ask me why I just smile and say.

You've got to …

Kiss an Angel Good Morning! …

and let her know you think about her when you're gone.

Kiss an Angel Good Morning …

and love her like the devil when you get back home.

Well, people may try to guess …

the secret of happiness …

but some of them never learn it's a simple thing.

The secret I'm speaking of …

is a woman and a man in love …

and the answer is in this song that I always sing.

You've got to …

Kiss an Angel Good Morning! …

and let her know you think about her when you're gone.

Kiss an Angel Good Morning! …

and love her like the devil when you get back home.

Kiss an Angel Good Morning! …

and let her know you think about her when you're gone.

Kiss an Angel Good Morning! …

and love her like the devil when you get back home."

"Hell yes … give us another one, Fry," Jack Jr. bellowed from behind the string of mules, clapping and hooting in appreciation.

"How about Roll on Mississippi?" Joe urged, requesting a second Charley Pride wrangler favorite.

The stock and the three young wranglers had heard many a *"calming"* verse bellowed from the lungs of Dick Fryhover, while on horseback, through the years. Tim, Jack Jr., and Joe found great *"comfort"* knowing that when Fry finished a song, within five minutes another would begin to ring out into the Bob Marshall Wilderness from their *"lifelong mentor"* sitting on the back of his beloved Spider.

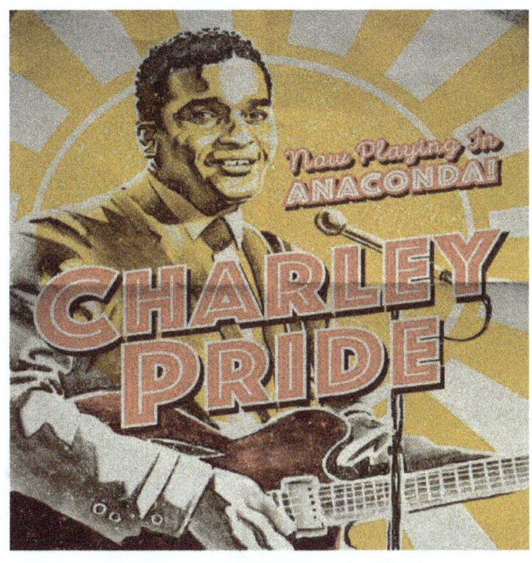

<u>Little Known Fact</u>: *Before Charley Pride became a famous Country Music Star, he was a semi-pro baseball pitcher for the "East Helena Smelterites" in 1960. Charley*

Around noon, the McMahons and Hanlons made it to the junction of Trail #202 and Trail #203. Trail #203 would lead them to their campsite at Indian Flats along the West Fork of the Sun River. Today, Trail #202 and Trail #203 combine to form a section of the Continental Divide Trail or CDT.

Jack stopped Romeo and slipped out of his saddle.

"We will grab lunch and take a quick break here. Be sure to secure your horses using the lead ropes attached to the halters, and not the reins of the bridles." Jack correctly instructed the group.

All nodded in agreement as they began to dismount to find a tree to secure their horse. Missy, Toots, Mike, and Tim politely helped the Hanlons tie up their horses, and grab the pre-made bologna and peanut butter and jelly sandwiches out of their saddle bags.

"Wow - only been two hours riding, Jack, and I feel like my hips are out of whack," Rollo said to Jack as he shook his legs out, bringing life back into them after the six-mile ride up to the junction.

"Takes a while getting used to – no doubt about that," Jack acknowledged.

"Did you see that young black bear up the tree to the left about a mile back?" Jack quietly asked Rollo, all the while making sure he was out of earshot of all the others.

"I sure didn't," Rollo replied.

"They are harmless. Almost like a pest back here at times. I did not stop to point him out because I did not want to cause an unnecessary stir," Jack Sr. stated.

"Do not worry about us, Jack. Peg and the girls can handle something like seeing that bear in the tree. Moving forward, feel free to completely immerse us in this wilderness. Hold nothing back," Rollo urged his former med student.

"Alright, will do. That is a great perspective. 100% discovery. We will have a wonderful time. Will not hold back, yet I promise Peg and the girls will never be placed in any true danger," Jack Sr. replied.

The next half hour consisted of refreshment and discovery. Upon quickly finishing their lunch, Mother Miss led the children down to the banks of the West Fork of the Sun, which they had just crossed over about two hundred yards back down the trail. Tadpoles were caught in drinking cups, a frog would end up in seven-year-old *"Curious Tim's"* saddlebags unbeknownst to all, and the Hanlon girls saw their first river otter as it fished for trout along the river's banks.

By 12:45 P.M., the group was mounted and ready to continue their journey into the West Fork of the Sun River Valley. About two miles up the trail, Oly had become bored with the walking pace Romeo had settled into as the lead horse.

The clever five-year-old realized that if she softly pulled back the reins, she could create a nice gap between her mare Lightning and the stallion Romeo. Once the gap was big enough for her liking, she would release pressure on the reins and give the mare a stern kick to the belly. Lightning would oblige and *"burst"* into a fast trot to catch up with Romeo.

Giggles of joy rang out from the children as the entire column of horses would follow Lightning's change of pace and join in the gap-changing trot. Jack Sr. ignored the game of *"**chase**"* that Oly had created behind him until Joanie decided her husband needed to intervene.

"Jack, that is enough. Stop pretending you do not know what is happening back here," Joanie demanded, five horses back, growing tired of the toll the change of pace was taking on her body.

"Oly, no more reining Lightning back, young lady. You heard your mother." Jack said, secretly grinning in appreciation of the joy Oly had created for the other children, while at the same time creating *"tooth jarring misery"* for the adult riders.

"Tommy told me to do it," she replied without hesitation as she caught up to her father.

As Jack turned around in the saddle, *"silent Tommy"* was peeking around Oly, shaking his head up and down in joyous agreement of her accusation.

"Looks like your saddle partner agrees with you. Regardless of who is at fault, we have all heard the boss. How about we keep Lightning up here on Romeo's tail until we get to the campsite?" Jack responded.

By late afternoon, Fry and the young wranglers had made it to the designated campsite along Indian Flats. Little was said as the packs were routinely unloaded from the stock.

"Tim and Joe get started getting the tents up between that group of pines over there," Fry instructed as he pointed to the tree line he had selected. "Jack and I will start getting the cook area completed."

Joe, being the youngest of the two, drew the *"short straw"* and quickly climbed fifteen feet up the pine they had selected to secure the tent rope to. Tim threw the *"hooked lash cinch"* end of the tent rope up to his partner. Securing the rope to the pine, Joe then transitioned down the tree as Tim Gleason kept the secured rope tight at ground level. Joe jogged over to the pine they had chosen to anchor the tent rope and waited for Tim to make his way over to him. Handing the taunt rope to Joe, Tim gave Joe a quick boost up to reach the first branch that hung eight feet off the ground out of his reach. Holding the taunt tent rope in his teeth, Joe grabbed the branch with both hands and effortlessly pulled his entire body up to the branch level. Joe ascended the rest of the way up the pine and *"anchor tied"* the tent rope securely.

As Joe hit the ground, Tim Gleason had already spread out the thirty-by-thirty black plastic tarp that would serve as the camp sleeping quarters. The boys quickly threw the tarp over the tent rope, forming an open-ended A-Frame sleeping quarters. The "common procedure" for securing the ground-level edges of the tent was to gather large numbers of river boulders to use as an anchoring system. Knowing, in about an hour, a "workforce" of nine *"boulder harvesting"* children would be arriving, the two young wranglers decided to use four sets of saddle bags to anchor the A-frame tent structure temporarily.

Guide Dick Fryhover had a *"specific"* backcountry cook area set up that he preferred at all camp spots. Jack Jr. and Fry built two prep tables out of the plywood kitchen pack boxes. The two of them then went to work on getting the grills set up to Fry's expectations by building a ***"square-shaped"*** fire pit with river boulders left behind by previous camp occupants.

<u>Left to Right</u>: *Son Charlie Mott, and Dick Fryhover cooking a breakfast of hotcakes and freshly caught trout for breakfast on the Dannaher River in The Bob in 1977.*

"Run down to the river and grab me four wide flat rocks to keep the food warm at the edge of the fire, and we'll have what we need here," Fry instructed Jack Jr.

Within five minutes, Jack Jr. returned with the four rocks, and the cook area of camp was complete, meeting Fry's standards.

Fry and Jack Jr. made their way over to the pack mules and horses, where Tim and Joe had begun the unsaddling process.

"Great choice fellas for the tack area," Fry complemented.

Joe and Tim nodded, acknowledging the praise. The two had hammered four ten-foot-long rails to a couple of nearby pines at various levels to hang the saddles and tack up off the ground in order to air out properly.

"How are you doing my friend?" Fry said to Chief as he reached under his belly to loosen the cinch of the Decker Packsaddle that the massive Appaloosa gelding had been carrying for the last nine hours on the trail.

Chief was a "_unique bareback or pack saddle only_" member of their herd. Jack and Fry had purchased Chief two years previous from an auction, believing they could "_convert_" the career rodeo "_bucking horse_" into a trail horse. That "_conversion_" to this point was an **EPIC** failure. Put a <u>riding-saddle</u> on Chief, then crawl up on his back = guaranteed to get your ass bucked off as multiple cowboys had before you. Put a <u>packsaddle</u> on Chief, load him up to your heart's desire = zero issues.

One evening in 1972, Jack McMahon Sr. pulled into the driveway of his Helena Valley home to a sight he could not believe. Missy was leading Chief by halter rope around the corral with Toots, Mike, Tim, and Oly safely on his back. **_Conclusion_**: Literally throw anything you want on Chief's back, as long as it is not a riding-saddle. The "_gentle giant_" became a unanimous favorite of the McMahon and Fryhover children.

Chief unexpectedly raised his head, throwing out a loud "_whinny_" into the calm Bob Marshall late afternoon air. As Fry pulled the packsaddle off Chief, he knew that "_welcome whinny_" signified the McMahon and Hanlon crew were nearby.

Sure enough, two minutes later, Romeo and Jack emerged from the tree-lined trail, marking the arrival of the remainder of the travelling party to the Indian Flats campsite.

CHAPTER 5: INDIAN FLATS CAMPSITE

The Indian Flats Campsite became remarkably busy with the arrival of the McMahon and Hanlon families. Guide Dick Fryhover assigned tasks to all, and the camp's complete construction came together quickly.

Fry, Joanie, and Dr. Peg Hanlon began preparing and cooking supper.

Missy, Mary, Martha, and Sarah were tasked with grabbing mantie tarps and laying them out along the ground within the A-frame tent that Joe and Tim Gleason had recently constructed. This would provide a "*dry*" base floor for the air mattresses and sleeping bags to rest upon.

As the tent floor was being constructed, Toots, Tim, Mike, Oly, and Tommy began gathering river boulders and placing them along the bottom edge of the plastic-tarped A-frame tent to anchor it down.

Jack McMahon Sr., Dr. C. Rollins Hanson, Tim Gleason, Jack McMahon Jr., and Joe McMahon unloaded and unsaddled the remaining stock.

Once they finished unsaddling all the mules and horses, the three young wranglers hopped on the bare backs of Lightning, Blaze, and Diala with the purpose of using them to "***halter ferry***" the rest of the stock across the West Fork of the Sun River to let out to pasture for the evening. By now, the other children had finished their "*tent tasks*" and came over to lend a hand to the young wranglers.

Rollo and Peg Hanlon stood watching in great fascination at the Sun River "***stock ferrying process***" that their three daughters had just been recruited to participate in.

"This sight is worth the trip right here," Peg exclaimed.

"The girls are not timid at all. Look at the smiles on their faces," Rollo replied.

Missy and Toots were the "***distributors***". Their role was to untie the stock from where they were tied at the campsite and give their lead rope to either Mike, Tim, Martha, Mary, or Sarah, who were labeled the "***runners***". These "***runners***" would then lead the stock down to the water, where the "***wranglers***" would lead two of the stock at a time by horseback across the Sun River to the other side. Once across, the "***wranglers***" would remove the halters from the stock they had just led across, allowing them to run free and graze on that side of the river.

What a sight to see ... Up the bank, Mike, Tim, Martha, Mary, and Sarah would hustle, grabbing the next horse or mule Missy and Toots distributed to them. Down the slope they would go, passing the lead ropes onto Tim Gleason, Jack Jr., or Joe at the river's edge.

To finish the process off, Tim Gleason, Jack Jr., and Joe attached a *"location bell"* around the necks of the three horses they were riding: Lightning, Blaze, and Diala. Once the bells were secure, they removed the halters, pointed them back across the Sun River, urging the three horses back across to join the rest of the herd.

Within fifteen minutes of beginning this **<u>ferrying process,</u>** all twenty-four head of stock were across the West Fork of the Sun River, grazing and *"rolling out"* a hard day's travel.

The purpose of *"pasturing"* the stock on the other side of the West Fork of the Sun River from camp was to prevent the "loose stock" from simply deciding to head back down the trail without them to Benchmark. The river functioned as a *"natural barrier"* Dick and Jack used to manage the stocks migratory movement while camped at Indian Flats. Imagine if the stock decided they wanted to head back to Benchmark, it would require them to cross the river and walk directly through the campsite, thus being detected immediately by all.

A great backcountry meal was had by all as nightfall came across Indian Flats. Campfire stories, marshmallow s'mores, and stargazing along the river's edge finished off a wonderful first evening.

The *"orchestra"* of stock bells across the river made for a relaxing *"chorus"* through the night as all slept very well.

Dick Fryhover quietly made his way out of the A-frame tent as the sun rose over Indian Flats. Jack McMahon Sr., wearing his fly jacket and carrying the case of fly rods, joined Fry at the edge of the campfire for a cup of morning coffee.

"Did not hear any critters last night around the campsite. How about you?" Jack inquired.

"Quiet as a church house mouse," his witty friend replied. "Hand me a couple of those rods, Jack. I will help you get them rigged up."

The two friends spent the next thirty minutes conversing and reliving wilderness adventures while getting the rods ready for the morning fish.

"Figure we cook up hot cakes, sausage, and eggs this first morning, Jack," Dick said as he came back from hanging the last rod from a tree along the path down to the river.

"Sounds great, Fry. I'll cook the eggs and sausage if you want to handle the hot cakes," Jack replied.

The *"smell of breakfast"* nudged the rest of the camp out of their warm sleeping bags.

The morning was spent fly fishing the West Fork of the Sun River. Tim Gleason and Jack Jr. *"guided"* Missy, Toots, Oly and the Hanlon girls about three-quarters of a mile up the river. Jack Sr. *"guided"* Rollo, Peg, and Joanie directly adjacent to the campsite. Dick Fryhover *"guided"* Joe, Tim, Mike, and Tommy down the river about a half mile.

Rainbow trout and whitefish hungrily smacked the Royal Wulff, Adams, and Caddis patterns tied to the end of the lines being cast up and down the river. A *"fan favorite"* brown trout also blessed a few anglers' lines on rare occasions. Joyful *"**I got one**"* outbursts of fish on the line filled the West Fork of the Sun River drainage that morning!

The three fishing parties met back at camp for lunch around noon. After lunch, Dick and Jack had a surprise for the children. They emerged from behind the designated saddle and tack area, carrying four black, fully inflated inner tubes.

"We're going tubing!" The children screamed in unison as they sprinted toward the A-frame tent to grab their swimsuits.

"A+, A+," Joanie smiled, clapping in praise of Jack and Dick. "Might have to sneak a couple bars of soap into that river with those tubes and children also."

"Thought you would approve. It was all Jack's idea," Dick said, shooting all the credit in his lifelong friend's direction.

"Oh, I'm sure that was all Jack," Joanie responded sarcastically, recognizing Fry's attempt to get Jack *"sweetheart points"* from his bride.

Within twenty minutes, the tubes and *"soap"* were in the water. The far shore had an *"audience"* of its own. The stock had heard the ruckus coming from the Sun River and curiously wandered up to get a peek.

The children took turns barreling down the river on the black inner tubes and *"produced"* quite an efficient system. Four children would tube down about one hundred and fifty yards into the arms of four other children that were posted across the river to serve as *"catchers,"* stopping their downward descent. The "catchers" would then run the tubes back up to the next four in line, and those that just tubed down would stay and *"catch."* Joanie *"cleverly"* snuck four bars of *"soap"* into the catchers' hands of this floating system now consisting of tubing, catching, running, and a *"washing up"* phase.

Two hours later, the children gathered back at the campsite for a snack, in need of another adventure to finish off the afternoon at Indian Flats.

A "**scavenger hunt**" was the final activity of the afternoon. Joanie and Peg put together two "even" rosters:

Team 1:	**Team 2:**
Missy	Mary
Martha	Sarah
Mike	Toots
Oly	Tim
Tommy	

Note: "Mother Missy" got the two babies of the trip, Oly and Tommy, to look after. Tim Gleason, Jack Jr., and Joe had purposely been excluded to allow them "fishing time" on their own.

Joanie and Peg had also put together a list of nature items to be gathered that included:

Three Tadpoles, Three snail shells, Three Bitterroot Wildflowers, Three Shooting Star Wildflowers

Three Pinecones, Ten Huckleberries, Ten Wild Strawberries, One Bird Feather, and One Animal Bone

The two teams attacked the "***scavenger hunt***" with completely different plans of action. Team 1 dashed out to the forest, and Team 2 started down at the river.

A bird feather was the most difficult item to find.

After an "*exhaustive search by all,*" Martha bound down the trail into camp, holding a bird feather, giving Team 1 the victory!

After dinner, the evening was spent fly fishing in the West Fork of the Sun River. The groups were *"purposely split"* up by family. Tim Gleason and Dick Fryhover *"guided"* the Hanlon family on the upstream section, while the McMahon family fished the lower section of the river.

"Throw it right up along that shoreline Toots," Jack instructed the only *lefty* in the family.

As soon as that Caddis pattern hit the soft current near the bank, a fourteen-inch brown trout smashed the fly. Toots brought that rod straight up and hooked him right on the upper lip. No slack was present in the line, and she had the brown right where she wanted him.

"ZZZZZZZZZZZZZZZ" the drag could be heard screaming out of that black Medley Reel as the brown dashed down the river.

"Keep the rod tip up and to the left, Toots. Let him take the line he wants off that reel." Jack bellowed as his daughter moved downstream, fighting the brown.

Two minutes later, twenty yards downstream from where she hooked the brown. The trout lay in her father's net, slowly treading water as she gently worked the Caddis from its upper lip.

"There you go, little buddy," Toots said as she released the brown back into the West Fork of the Sun River.

"You did great!" Jack Sr. exclaimed, reaching down to help her back up to her feet.

"Time to do it again!" she said, flashing her father with a smile as wide as that river.

"Looks like you got that smile you wanted," Joanie shot down to Jack Sr.

"I have been given ten of them tonight, and I will take ten more if the fish are willing," her husband said, flashing a smile of his own back upstream.

About a half a mile up the West Fork of the Sun River, the Hanlons were hauling in rainbow and brown trout left and right.

"Cast that Wulff to the left of where you just saw that fish rise, Sarah, and let it drift down to him," Dick Fryhover instructed.

Sarah sent a smooth *"splash less"* cast just as instructed. She stared intently at the Royal Wulff, stripping the line of excess slack as it made its way down to where that trout had just risen.

"Bang!" That rainbow hit that fly like a hammer on a nail. Sarah lifted that rod tip up like an old pro, setting the hook by squeezing her right thumb on the line where the corked shaft of the rod sits above the reel, eliminating any slack in the line.

"You are not going to be able to get him on the reel. Just keep that thumb tight on the line and strip him in, Sarah," Rollo calmly *guided* his daughter.

Sarah calmly battled the thirteen-inch rainbow, stripping him into the shoreline where Fry waited with the net.

"I thought Dick was the guide here, Rollin?" Peg jabbed at her husband as Sarah finished landing the beautifully colored trout.

"I must admit those detailed instructions surprised myself. I guess you have been incorrect for the past twenty-four years of our marriage. This is indisputable proof that I am one hell of a listener," Rollo stated with immense pride.

Fry quickly threw a compliment in Rollo's direction, "You're now a certified fly fisherman, Doc. Congratulations."

The two doctors and Fry all shared a joyous laugh as Sarah released the rainbow back into the river.

Large numbers of trout were caught over the next hour. Slowly and methodically, the two families fished their way back to the campsite before darkness fell upon them.

The campfire that night was "full" of laughter, as memories of the day rang into the night air along Indian Flats and the West Fork of the Sun River.

CHAPTER 6:
TABLE ROCK

The morning of August 16, 1973, came early to the campsite and all its inhabitants. The plan for the day was to make a ***"day ride"*** up to the Table Rock area below the Chinese Wall, about seven miles up Trail #203/Continental Divide Trail.

"Tim, Jack, and Joe, after breakfast, scoot across the river and start fetching the horses and mules. The rest of us will grab them from you on this side of the river and get them saddled up." Dick Fryhover instructed

"Got it Fry," the three wranglers replied in unison as they stuffed French toast, hash browns, and scrambled eggs into their hungry bellies.

Fifteen minutes later, Tim Gleason, Jack McMahon Jr., and Joe McMahon were wading across the chilly waters of the West Fork of the Sun River.

"Hey look! There's three deer," Joe pointed out downriver.

Sure enough, a doe and two fawns were crossing the river about fifty yards below them.

"I feel like that doe. Leading two misfits into the unknown," Tim Gleason teased back to Jack Jr. and Joe.

"Clueless leading greatness, right Tim?" Joe shot back laughingly, attempting to turn the "*ignorance title*" in Tim's direction.

Once across, the wranglers found the herd of stock about three hundred yards upriver in the trees thanks to the "*location bells*" Lightning, Blaze, and Diala were wearing around their necks.

Joe had brought a canvas bucket filled with pellets across the river with him. Once the stock was in sight, he began shaking the bucket. The stock quickly began to make its way to the three wranglers in hopes of getting one of those tasty pellets as a breakfast snack. Thanks to the canvas bucket filled with pellets "trick," getting halters on Lightning, Blaze, and Diala was completed with ease.

Swinging up onto the backs of these three horses, the wranglers made their way down to the Sun River's edge, where they had dropped a pile of halters about ten minutes earlier upon their crossing. Behind them, the rest of the stock followed in hopes of obtaining a *"coveted pellet"* from that canvas bag Joe was shaking aboard Lightning.

Joe spread pellets out along the shore of the river. The spread of pellets created a stock line. The three wranglers then haltered the remaining herd.

Mounting back up on Lightning, Blaze, and Diala, the wranglers led stock across the Sun River. Dick Fryhover and the rest of the camp inhabitants were there as promised, with open arms to lead the stock up to be saddled for the ride up to Table Rock.

"Tie all the stock we are not taking with us to those pines back behind the tent area over there," Fry said, pointing to the pines he had chosen to provide shade for the stock.

"Excuse my curiosity, Dick. Having a tough time understanding why all the stock was brought back across the river?" Rollo said as he began throwing a saddle on the mare Malibu for Peg.

"That is a great question," acknowledged Dick Fryhover. "Horses are similar to humans. When the herd gets separated, those left behind have an *"instinctive need"* to re-unite. We bring them over and secure them because within an hour of our leaving, they will either be heading up the trail to Table Rock to find us or heading back to Benchmark."

"Fascinating, Fry. Thank you for the clarification," Rollo replied in appreciation.

Within an hour, the horses were saddled. The trek up to Table Rock from the campsite at Indian Flats would be a "steady" seven-mile climb.

Five miles into the ride, the crossing at Burnt Creek was a welcome sight to all. The thirsty stock buried their noses in the refreshing water, recovering from the steep climb.

"Be sure all canteens are full of water. No water available beyond this point up to Table Rock," Dick Fryhover shouted out to all as he knelt next to the water filling his canteen.

The horses and humans were all properly hydrated. Thus, signaling Fry to give Spider a nudge with his boots, and off they went back up the trail.

Within thirty minutes, the Chinese Wall began to *"**show off**"* its beauty up trail on the horizon. The limestone structure made the last two miles of the morning journey pass quickly.

By 1:00 P.M., all members of the riding party were dismounted in awe at Table Rock.

Jack Mahon found a *"designated shade"* area to tie the horses to in a group of tall pines for the remainder of the afternoon.

Once the stock was secured and their saddle cinches loosened to give comfort and prevent sores, the group gathered at the big flat rock, nicknamed Table Rock by Dick Fryhover, to enjoy lunch.

"Look, girls, there's a deer grazing," Peg Hanlon said, pointing to the prairie below them.

Within ten minutes, the curious young buck had grazed his way to within fifteen yards of the lunch site.

Sarah and Toots stood up and slowly made their way to about ten yards away from the curious two-point buck. Both girls stood statuesque and held out the remainder of their peanut butter and jelly sandwiches, offering to share with the young deer.

To the surprise of the "silent" crowd, the cautious buck slowly crept towards the ten-year- old courageous duo.

Joanie McMahon *"firmly squeezed"* the arm of Jack Sr., silently insisting that he stop the developing situation with this curious, horned wild creature. Despite the *"maternal cue"* to intervene, Jack *"bravely"* chose to let the children ***"live the moment."***

Sure enough, the buck leaned his head out in complete ***"trUst,"*** taking Sarah's peanut butter and jelly sandwich from her inviting hand. The buck cautiously backed away from his newfound lunch partners and bound smoothly to the edge of the timber with the prized snack firmly in his mouth.

A roar of "Wow ... No way ... That is so cool ... That did not just happen ... Unbelievable ..." words and statements of fascination echoed in from the astonished onlookers.

"Did you see that? ... Did you set that?" Sarah and Toots bellowed with joy as they ran in unison into the open arms of their mother's Peg, and Joanie.

"That was amazing. I am so proud of you!" Peg whispered into Sarah's ear.

"That looked so fun. You are so brave!" stated Joanie, pulling Toots into her loving arms.

"Don't think we'll see that again in our lifetimes," Fry shot out to Jack Sr. and Rollo.

"We agreed on 100% discovery, right, Rollo?" Jack Sr. reminded his mentor.

"We sure did, Jack," exclaimed Rollo. "Whichever one of you "*planted*" that tame buck up here, I owe you big time," he added.

"You will have to take that up with a higher power than either of us, Doc. Have not figured out a way to get a live deer to ride a pack saddle for twenty miles in the backcountry yet," responded Fry in laughter.

The rest of the afternoon was one of exploration and appreciation of the magnificent Chinese Wall. "***The Bob***" delivered as only nature can for the next four hours.

5:15 P.M. is what it read on Dick Fryhover's watch—time to head back down the trail to Indian Flats. The sun sets around 8:30 P.M. this time of year. By leaving now, it should put them back in camp comfortably by no later than 7:45 P.M.

The ride to Table Rock was a "*steep ascent*," which meant the ride back down to camp would be a "*steep descent*." Riding trail horses for extended periods of time downhill can create "*nasty cinch sore rubs*" on the belly area of the horses. Therefore, Jack Sr. and Fry instructed the adults and older children to "*walk and lead*" their horses until the trail began to flatten out.

CHAPTER 7:
THE FALL

Five miles down the inclined trail, Joe McMahon had grown tired of walking and decided to hop back into the saddle aboard his gelding Cocoa. Joe quickly caught up with Oly and Tommy, sharing a saddle aboard the *"steady"* mare Lightning. Jack McMahon Sr. was leading the stallion Romeo in front of Oly and Tommy as instructed by Joanie in the car ride up from Benchmark.

Two miles up from the Indian Flats campsite, there was a series of shallow creeks that crisscrossed Trail #203. Horses would, on occasion, prefer to "hop" over these narrow creeks rather than wade through them.

Lightning sure enough *"hopped"* over the first creek she came to, and to the surprise of Joe, Tommy came tumbling off behind her.

Jack McMahon Sr. heard a loud "***THUMP***" behind him and stopped immediately on the trail. As he turned back up the trail, he noticed Joe frantically dismounting Cocoa.

"I think Tommy's hurt," Joe hollered, moving quickly to his brother's side.

Jack McMahon let out a loud "***alert whistle***" before hustling back to help Tommy.

Dick Fryhover was in the lead, and Tim Gleason had assumed the end position of the trail ride for the return to camp. The "***alert whistle***" instinctively froze both men in their tracks. Something "*unexpected*" had just taken place between the two of them along the trail.

Tommy lay there on the edge of the creek, out cold.

"Tommy, Tommy, are you ok?" Jack Sr. said as he knelt to the level of his unconscious son.

No response.

"Tommy, Tommy, are you ok?" Joe chimed in, trying to get his brother to respond.

Jack Sr. checked Tommy's vitals and was relieved that a pulse was present and breathing was confirmed.

"What happened Joe?" Jack Sr. calmly questioned him as he lifted the unconscious child into his arms.

"Lightning hopped the creek, and Tommy fell off into the creek bed. Looks as if he had fallen asleep riding behind Oly," Joe replied, clearly shaken.

By now, Rollo had made his way up to the injury site.

"Let me take a look Jack," Dr. Hanlon said as he began to examine Tommy's scalp for signs of injury gently.

"There is a big red knot forming here, Jack. Rub your hand across this area. I am assuming there had to have been blunt force trauma to that area," Dr. Hanlon said as he pointed to the injured area on the right side of Tommy's scalp.

"I heard one hell of a ***THUMP,*** Rollo. Hitting his head on one of those rocks on the edge of the creek is my initial assessment," Dr. Jack McMahon replied as he felt the injured area Dr. Hanlon had pointed out.

The boy began to moan as his eyes opened, looking up at his father.

"Boy, am I glad to see those brown eyes," Jack Sr. joyously cried out to Tommy, giving his son a comforting kiss on the forehead.

Tommy lethargically tried to communicate with his father, but could not be understood.

"Joe, run! Grab that small black flashlight from my saddle bags," Jack instructed as five-year-old Oly clung with concern to her father's leg after climbing down from Lightning.

Joe returned quickly with the black flashlight as instructed. Jack flashed the light into Tommy's eyes, checking for dilated pupils.

Without saying a word to one another, Jack and Rollo knew the boy was in trouble due to the enlargement of his pupils.

Jack Jr. held Spider's reins for Dick as he made his way back up the trail to check on the "*alerted*" situation. Joanie and Peg dismounted and joined him as they made their way back to Jack Sr.

Joanie immediately "*sensed*" the concern in Jack and Rollo's eyes upon getting back to Tommy.

"What happened, Jack? Tell me he is going to be all right, Jack," said Joanie's voice, cracking as tears began to flow down her cheeks.

"Lightning hopped the creek, Joanie, and Tommy tumbled off. We believe he hit his head on one of these rocks. He was unconscious for a couple of minutes, but just came around," he replied, scooting close to Joanie and putting Tommy in her arms.

"Mommy's here," Joanie said softly, lifting Tommy up to her chin to comfort him.

"Definite concussion symptoms. Pupils are enlarged and are not reacting to the light appropriately. I am concerned," Dr. Jack McMahon said, holding no facts of the assessment back from his bride.

The father Jack McMahon's internal emotions were silently tearing him apart with concern for Tommy. Yet, he knew that the surgeon Dr. Jack McMahon's "*decisive expertise*" must be his personal "*focal point*" moving forward.

Jack McMahon Sr., Rollo Hanlon, and Peg Hanlon will be referred to as Dr. Jack McMahon, Dr. C. Rollins Hanlon, and

Dr. Peg Hanlon as this medical emergency runs its course throughout the remaining pages of this book.

The "***harsh** reality of this moment*" is that Tommy's life will depend ***ONLY*** on their "**professional knowledge and skill set,**" not "**paternal *love or unwavering support*.**"

The three Doctors, Joanie, and Dick Fryhover discussed a plan of action moving forward. Getting Tommy back to camp became priority number one.

"Jack, throw Tommy and yourself on Romeo. I will lead Romeo behind Spider. This way, you can keep Tommy stable in both arms for the remainder of the trip down. I will have Tim Gleason lead Lightning and Oly down, also Joanie," Fry suggested.

The group agreed, and within five minutes, all were mounted and moving down the trail.

The next hour on the trail would "*reveal*" the true prognosis of this head injury.

All three doctors internally felt the "*final prognosis*" would lead to an "***act***" that could not be "***attempted***" anywhere but the campsite at Indian Flats.

Over the next hour, Tommy fell in and out of consciousness. The amount of time he remained conscious would "*shrink*" between the episodes. Tommy's eyes had also turned to the right and upward, along with showing some partial rigidity. The "*prognosis*" the three doctors feared was coming to full fruition in Dr. Jack McMahon Sr.'s arms.

It was 8:15 PM by the time they made it back to the Indian Flats campsite. Day was quickly becoming night over the West Fork of the Sun River, adding another *"obstacle"* to this emergency they had found themselves in.

Tim Gleason, Jack Jr., and Joe were tasked with getting the stock unsaddled and completing the "ferrying" process across the Sun River to pasture.

Dr. Jack McMahon, Dr. C. Rollins Hanlon, and Dr. Peg Hanlon did a *"deep examination"* of the *"currently unconscious"* Tommy lying on the camp table Fry had constructed out of the plywood pack boxes two days previous. Tommy's breathing was becoming noticeably *"heavy."*

Joanie McMahon and Dick Fryhover observed and listened intently.

Dr. Jack McMahon shared with the group Tommy's current pattern of a short conscious state, then falling into an elongated unconscious state. The fact that the child's unconscious states were lasting longer and longer *"clarified"* to all three surgeons that the head injury would *"eventually"* require surgery to relieve the pressure caused by a cranial hematoma, skull fracture, or some other form of internal trauma to the cranial region.

How much time did they have? What was the best *"plan of action"* to get Tommy to a hospital ALIVE?

Three choices were discussed:

1. **"Place Tommy"** in Jack Sr.'s arms and have Fry lead them out through the night, fifteen miles to

Benchmark at a *"walk pace."* Upon arrival, transfer into one of the vehicles and get Tommy to the Emergency Room at Deaconess Hospital in Great Falls, two and a half hours up the road.

Approximate arrival in Great Falls: 9:00 A.M. the next morning.

Treatment rendered to Tommy: None

2. **"*Stably Pack*"** Tommy out of The Bob in one of the saddle paniers on a pack horse through the night, fifteen miles to Benchmark at the same *"walk pace."* Upon arrival, transfer into one of the vehicles and get Tommy to the Emergency Room at Deaconess Hospital in Great Falls, two and a half hours up the road.

Approximate arrival in Great Falls: 9:00 A.M. the next morning.

Treatment rendered to Tommy: None

3. **"Cranial Burr Hole"** field surgery performed here at Indian Flats to relieve the pressure building in Tommy's brain. Immediately send Dick Fryhover and Tim Gleason on horseback to Benchmark at a *"gallop/trot pace."* Transfer into one of the vehicles and get to the town of Augusta, fifty minutes away and phone in an emergency helicopter to fly in and take Tommy out by air.

Approximate arrival in Great Falls: 6:00 A.M. the next morning.

Treatment rendered to Tommy: Cranial "Burr hole" field surgery.

Dr. Jack McMahon, Dr. C. Rollins Hanlon, and Dr. Peg Hanlon did not believe Tommy would survive another three to four hours without a "***surgical intervention.***"

At a minimum, it would take five hours just to get Tommy out to a vehicle at Benchmark in Jack's arms or in the pack saddle panier. Field surgery in the dark on the trail, not if but when, would be impossible.

That imminent "***surgical intervention***" would need to be done here at Indian Flats.

Upon deep discussion, **Option 3, Cranial Burr Hole** field surgery, was the unanimous decision.

With Tommy in her arms, Joanie tearfully made her way to the A-Frame tent. The thought of losing another child was tearing a hole in her heart. Dr. Peg Hanlon carried Oly in silence behind her.

WHAT NEEDS TO GET DONE:

1. Dick Fryhover and Tim Gleason would ride out immediately and **"*secure*"** a rescue helicopter that would bring Tommy out to Deaconess Medical Hospital in Great Falls.
2. Assign roles to tasks 3 through 6 listed below.
3. Find a sufficient area to land the helicopter safely.
4. Build a **"*signal fire*"** at the landing area sight large enough for the helicopter to locate from the air as it would make its way up the West Fork of the Sun River in the darkness. This fire was to be lit at 3:00 A.M. and must remain lit until the chopper arrived or daybreak, whichever came first. This would require that substantial amounts of dry wood be collected.
5. Once it would be apparent that the helicopter has located the landing site, the FIRE MUST BE PUT OUT before the helicopter lands. This would require a "significant stash" of water to be present at the site of the signal fire. The rotors on the helicopter could create strong enough winds to spread the "signal fire"

into an uncontrollable forest fire if not put out before the helicopter touches down at the landing site.

6. Have a "definitive" plan to transport Tommy from the campsite to the designated landing site of the helicopter. The child would need to remain in a *"flat immobile"* position post-surgery.

7. *"Delay"* the field surgery as long as possible due to the realistic fact that, in the *"best case scenario,"* from an elapsed time standpoint, the chopper would arrive around 3:00 A.M. ... Assuming all goes right for Dick Fryhover and Tim Gleason.

Note: The longer the surgeons "***SAFELY***" wait to relieve the pressure in Tommy's skull, the better chance he has to survive post-surgery and make it to Great Falls. The small emergency medical kit they have to care for the child post-surgery properly will begin to get *"stretched"* thin as soon as they complete the cranial *"burr hole"* procedure.

CHAPTER 8:
"MIDNIGHT RIDE"

Dick Fryhover hustled down to Tim Gleason, who was dutifully unsaddling the stock.

Fry tapped the young wrangler on the shoulder, "I need you to ride out to Benchmark with me tonight. Tommy is not going to make it out of here unless we can get a helicopter here to evacuate him. I need another rider with me in case something happens to one of the horses or me. One of us **MUST** get that chopper in here."

"You got it, Fry. What horses do you want me to saddle?" Tim Gleason responded unfazed.

"Throw your saddle on Charley, and I will throw mine on that young mare Gerado," Fry instructed. "They did not make the trip up the mountain with us today. Those two quarter horses have the "*fresh legs*" we need to get this done. This is a hackamore night, Tim, no bridles necessary for this trip!"

"I'm on it," Tim said as he began to move towards the tack area.

"Tim," Dick Fryhover said, catching Tim's attention. "Do not say a word to the other children. They are pretty shaken up. No need to make things worse. Jack and Joanie will handle all updates regarding Tommy's injury."

Tim Gleason flashed Fry a thumbs-up as he hustled down to grab the saddles and hackamores.

A hackamore is a *"bitless"* bridle. Fry chose hackamores instead of bridles to encourage Charley and Gerado to *"shag ass"* down the West Fork of the Sun River trail with limited restriction.

Within five minutes, Charley and Gerado were saddled. Charley was a seasoned trail horse, while Gerado was a former racehorse that was still *"adjusting"* to her new life role as a trail horse.

"You are going to have to lead the way, Tim. It will be pitch black in fifteen minutes. This mare is not ready to lead us down that dark trail. ***Charley's got this, Tim, just give him his head***. Touch those reins as little as possible; in fact, I recommend you wrap them around the saddle horn and let him go." Fry instructed as he put his left foot in the stirrup and pulled himself onto Gerado.

"Got it Fry. Let's get us a chopper!" Tim responded with confidence as he dug his boots into Charley, sending the two men barreling out of the campsite towards Benchmark.

Within minutes, darkness had overcome The West Fork of the Sun River trail just as Fry promised. A thick cloud cover hid the only light the two riders could have used to aid them in their journey.

Charley moved down the trail as if it were the middle of the day. The gelding's pace fluctuated masterfully between a hard trot and a solid gallop, depending on the terrain he instinctively assessed beneath his pounding hooves.

Gerado's speed traits *"pushed"* Charley like a tailwind towards the Benchmark Trailhead. Tim could feel the mare's breath on the back of his saddle and could not help but wonder to himself if Fry *"knew"* this would happen by purposely placing the fleet-footed Gerado behind Charley.

The West Fork of the Sun River's current provided a *"calming"* to the ears of both riders as they rushed down the shoreline trail in a focused silence.

Around 11:30 P.M., two and a half hours after leaving Indian Flats, Charley and Gerado's steel-shod hooves pounded across the wooden bridge at the Benchmark Trailhead. This same sixteen-mile trek from Indian Flats had taken them seven hours just two days earlier.

Tim Gleason pulled back hard on Charley's reins as they arrived at the Benchmark Ranger Station.

Dick Fryhover barreled off Gerado, handing Tim Gleason the mare's reins to hold as he flew up the steps of the uninhabited cabin. Fry banged on the door frantically, hollering for assistance.

"The cabin is locked up! There is no one here, Tim. We are going to need to get to the Sheriff in Augusta," Fry exclaimed as he hustled down the steps and mounted back up on Gerado.

Tim Gleason tossed Dick Fryhover Gerado's reins, and off they went at a full gallop back down the trail.

Tim guided Charley into the corral area at Benchmark about a quarter mile down from the vacant Ranger Station.

"Try to get us as close as you can to the vehicles," Fry hollered ahead to Tim.

As commanded, Tim Gleason reined Charley to the closest hitching post near Fry's white Chevy suburban *"Brophy."*

Both men frantically dismounted the heavily breathing quarter horses that were drenched with sweat, and without hesitation, tied them off to the hitching post.

"We do not have time to unsaddle them, Tim. Grab your canteen, loosen Charley's saddle cinch a notch and let's get up the road." Fry hastily instructed the young wrangler.

Within two minutes of their arrival, Dick Fryhover was guiding Brophy *"**full pedal**"* up the gravel dirt road between Benchmark and Augusta to fetch a helicopter for the young child he had affectionately bestowed the nickname *"Tom Slick."*

"Tim, I am going to need to guide the helicopter into Indian Flats. Charley and Gerado may not make it through the night. We rode the guts out of the two of them. When you get back here in the morning, if they are dead, hook them up to one of the pickups and drag them out of the corral area. Get them far enough out of there where the *"critters"* will not create a problem for the other outfitters in the corral area," Dick Fryhover decisively relayed the possible fate of the two quarter horses and instructions to the seventeen-year-old wrangler.

"Will do, Fry," Tim Gleason responded, clasping to the edge of his seat and door handle, praying for his own life as Fry *"sped out of control"* up the gravel road towards Augusta.

Dick Fryhover made the fifty-minute trip to Augusta in thirty minutes.

Upon arrival, Dick Fryhover was able to track down a local sheriff deputy who ***"attempted"*** to assist them in trying to secure the helicopter to go into the West Fork of the Sun River to evacuate Tommy.

The hospitals in Missoula and Great Falls, Montana, were the only hospitals big enough in 1973 to provide emergency helicopter service.

Despite Dick Fryhover's "*plea for assistance*," both hospitals' medical dispatchers informed Dick Fryhover that their helicopters were not equipped for emergency rescue missions into the wilderness areas of Montana at night or in daylight hours.

Deaconess Hospital in Great Falls suggested Dick Fryhover reach out to Malmstrom Air Force Base, located in Great Falls. Malmstrom had a helicopter squadron with helicopters that were better equipped to handle the emergency with which he was facing.

The sheriff deputy helped Fry contact the medical dispatcher at Malmstrom Air Force Base.

Dick Fryhover laid out the Indian Flats emergency with "*concise detail*" as the medical dispatcher listened in to the call and "*noted*" all the pertinent information.

"We do not have **clearance** to fly into the Bob Marshall Wilderness Area in the dark, sir. We will have to wait for daylight to send the chopper in to evacuate the boy," the dispatcher informed Fry.

"I don't know if Tommy will survive ..." Dick Fryhover began to plead.

"I need to clarify one thing with you. Did you say Dr. C. Rollins Hanlon, the Executive Director of the American College of Surgeons, is assisting at the campsite?" the medical dispatcher interrupted Fry for clarification.

"Yes. Dr. C. Rollins Hanlon and his wife, Dr. Peg Hanlon are at the campsite with Dr. Jack McMahon, and they were preparing to perform field surgery on his son Tommy when I exited the campsite. Those three surgeons felt that if we do not get the boy evacuated as soon as possible upon the conclusion of the surgery that his chances for survival will decrease rapidly." Fry pleaded in clarification to the Malmstrom dispatcher.

Dr. C. Rollin Hanlon's name had struck a nerve with the medical dispatcher. The dispatcher had just attended a medical conference where Dr. Hanlon was a guest speaker, in Great Falls. The **_nationally respected_** surgeon had mentioned in his talk that he was going to take a trip into the Bob Marshall Wilderness with one of his former students.

"Allow me a couple of minutes to relay your emergency to the pilots and crew," the medical dispatcher informed Fry.

Unbeknownst to Fry, his plea for help had also been heard at the Malmstrom Medical Dispatch Center by Pilot Capt. Buck Buchanan, and his copilot, Lt. James M. McKee.

CHAPTER 9:
TASKS TO COMPLETE

Dr. Jack McMahon brought the two families together at the campfire ten minutes after the Dick Fryhover and Tim Gleason *"accelerated departure."*

With *"unwavering"* personal strength and elite detail, he laid out to all what needed to be done moving forward through the night that lay ahead of them.

"Great job getting the stock across the river to the pasture. Your mothers are with Tommy and Oly in the tent. We sent Fry and Tim Gleason down to Benchmark in hopes that they could get a helicopter to the campsite later tonight to take Tommy out to the hospital in Great Falls, where he can get the help he needs. There are a few tasks we will need to complete to get Tommy out of here safely on that chopper. This is going to take everything you've got." Dr. Jack McMahon urged as the Hanlon and McMahon children nodded back intently.

"We will need to gather wood and build a *"signal fire"* large enough for the helicopter to recognize as it flies over the campsite. Three hundred yards down the trail, there is an open *"ridge area"* we will use as the landing site for the helicopter and signal fire location. We will need to fill all saddle canteens and the eight canvas buckets with water. Once we have the water, I will take you up on that ridge where I need you to gather as much dry wood as possible for the signal fire. Each of you grab the flashlights out of your backpacks or saddle bags and meet me down at the river." Dr. McMahon instructed.

By 10:00 P.M., Dr. Jack McMahon, Martha, Mary, Jack Jr., Joe, and Missy were carrying buckets and canteens of water down the trail to the designated *"open ridge landing site."*

Sarah, Toots, Mike, and Tim were left behind at the tent to be put to bed by Dr. Peg Hanlon and Joanie McMahon. Dr. McMahon did not feel comfortable leaving those children, aged ten and under, up on that ridge all night securing and lighting the *"signal fire."*

Dr. Hanlon stayed back in camp **"preparing and sterilizing"** the supplies and tools they would need to relieve the deadly pressure building up in the child's skull.

Dr. Jack McMahon *"purposely avoided"* the fact that an emergency field surgery at the campsite would be taking place within the next couple of hours. Currently, the children "believed" Tommy was going to stay in the caring arms of Joanie in the tent until a helicopter arrived to evacuate him. Dr. McMahon felt that the picture of "maternal security" each of them were leaving the campsite with, or crawling into their sleeping bags with, was the appropriate *"representation of the situation"* they needed in their young, concerned minds.

Once at the landing site, Dr. McMahon selected the site for the *"signal fire."*

Dr. McMahon then proceeded to instruct and help the children begin building the signal fire from the dry wood that was prevalent on the edges of the open ridge line.

"Missy, I am going to leave this pocket watch of mine with you. At 3:00 A.M., the *"signal fire"* must be ignited, no earlier, no later. Do not let this fire go out until the helicopter arrives or daybreak takes over this ridgeline," Dr. Jack McMahon instructed his *"trUstworthy"* fourteen-year-old daughter and the four other children.

"Got it, Dad," Missy reassured her father, taking the pocket watch out of his hand.

Doc helped Martha, Mary, Jack Jr., Joe, and Missy spread the canteens and canvas buckets filled with water in a large circle around the designated *"signal fire"* location.

Dr. McMahon then focused his attention on the procedure that would be needed to put the signal fire out before the helicopter began its descent onto the landing site.

"Once the helicopter **"recognizes"** the signal fire, it will stop its trajectory up the river valley and turn around heading back in your direction, signaling that it **"has located"** the landing site. As soon as that chopper gets turned back in your direction, quickly begin to douse the *"signal fire"* out," Doc explained in decisive detail.

No sooner had Dr. McMahon put the children back on task, gathering the dry wood for the signal fire, than he heard footsteps quickly coming up the ridge in their direction.

"Jack, I need to talk with you about something," Dr. C. Rollins Hanlon said out of breath.

Dr. McMahon made sure to meet with Dr. Hanlon out of *"earshot"* of the children.

"It is time. I'm sorry, Jack. Tommy's digressing quickly. His right pupil is not responding to light at all, and I believe his breathing pattern has fallen into a Cheyne-Stokes respiration pattern." Dr. Hanlon delivered the heart-piercing news.

Cheyne-Stokes respiration is a breathing pattern characterized by cycles of increased and decreased breathing, followed by periods of apnea. It is often associated with serious medical conditions such as congestive heart failure, stroke, brain injury, or end-of-life stages. ***In the context of head injury trauma***, Cheyne-Stokes respiration can be a sign of brain injury, particularly if it is rapid and followed by periods of apnea. *(umaryland.edu>educational_pearls)*

Without hesitation, Dr. Jack McMahon hollered up the ridge, "Jack, I need you to come with me for a few minutes."

Sixteen-year-old Jack Jr. hustled down to his father, and the three rapidly made the trek back down to the Indian Flats campsite.

Upon entering the campsite area, Dr. Jack McMahon **"transformed"** from **father** to **surgeon** immediately.

"Jack, we are going to need to operate on Tommy, and I need you to hold the kerosene lantern for Dr. Hanlon and myself. There is a bucket of hot water on the grill at the campfire. Use the ladle and soap I left there and get your hands cleaned up as best you can," Dr. McMahon instructed his son on his way to the A-frame tent to grab Tommy from Joanie.

"Peg, I think it's best if you stay with Joanie and act as the relay of medical information for her as we work on Tommy,"

Dr. Jack McMahon suggested as he made his way into the tent.

"I agree Jack," Dr. Peg Hanlon acknowledged.

Jack McMahon, the ***"father/husband,"*** caught eye contact with his grieving wife as he reached to take Tommy from her trembling arms.

"You will hold Tommy again, Joanie," Dr. Jack McMahon, the **"surgeon,"** reassured his terrified bride.

Joanie pulled Tommy up to her lips and then slowly set him in Dr. Jack McMahon's *"trUsted"* hands.

CHAPTER 10:
"*TRUST*"

The medical dispatcher at Malmstrom Air Force Base in Great Falls began to relay emergency information to Pilot Capt. Buck Buchanan, and Copilot James M. McKee.

"We heard the entire conversation on the speaker," Buck Buchanan interrupted. "That boy has no chance if we don't saddle up and get him out of there immediately. Those three surgeons relayed medical information to Fryhover in that detail because they knew this kid was in some serious trouble. The two of us have flown many a night mission in our careers, James. I say we get him out of there."

"We don't have clearance, Buck. Consequences will come the second we lift that bird up in the dark out on that pad." Lt. James M. McKee cautioned.

"I will wear those **"consequences"** with pride on this uniform, James. That *"signal fire"* will be lit from O-three hundred to daybreak like Fryhover is promising. We are going in. Put me on the horn with Fryhover or that deputy." Buck Buchanan instructed the medical dispatcher.

"Who am I speaking with?" Capt. Buck Buchanan asked as he picked up the telephone receiver.

"This is Dick Fryhover," the voice on the other end responded.

"Dick, my name is Capt. Buck Buchanan. My crew and myself are going to fly in and get that boy out of The Bob. We are going to leave the base ASAP, yet I am going to need your help. Can you guide us into that campsite?" the pilot asked Fry.

"Absolutely," Dick Fryhover responded.

"There is a grass airstrip on the outside of town, in Augusta. It is about O-two hundred now, can you meet us there at O-three hundred?" Capt. Buck Buchanan requested.

"I will see you in an hour, Captain," Dick Fryhover gratefully shot back.

With that, the call went dead on the other end, and Dick Fryhover breathed a "*short-lived*" sigh of relief.

It hit Fry as soon as that breath left his lungs.

Dick Fryhover's mind began racing as he silently said to himself, "Who is going to guide that helicopter back in from Indian Flats? I will be hopping off, and Jack Sr., as planned, will be riding in with Tommy as the two of us had discussed by the campfire four hours earlier."

"Does Bob Duncan reside here in Augusta?" Fry asked the sheriff deputy as an idea popped into his mind.

"Yes, Ranger Duncan lives about two miles outside of town. Why?" the deputy responded.

"I'm going to need him to ride the chopper in with us. I am getting off at the campsite and being replaced by Dr. McMahon and the boy. They will need me there at the campsite to pack them out. Bob Duncan's expertise of that Sun River drainage would be of immense value to the pilots as that bird makes its way back to Great Falls," Fry informed the sheriff deputy.

"I will call him immediately and pick him up on my way to the airstrip," the deputy responded.

Bob Duncan was the Sun River District Ranger that Dick Fryhover encountered many times along the West Fork of the Sun River Trail over the past two summers.

As Dick Fryhover and Tim Gleason sat waiting for the helicopter to arrive from Malmstrom. Fry admitted that his *"insides"* were turning circles. Dick Fryhover had flown in a few helicopters while serving in the Korean War from 1950 to 1953; those *"night flight"* memories were beginning to flash back rapidly. (**_Photo_** = *Dick Fryhover in Korea)*

Sure enough, at 3:00 A.M., the helicopter touched down on that remote grassy airstrip on the outskirts of Augusta, Montana.

Dick Fryhover handed Brophy's keys to the young wrangler sitting silently in the passenger seat and said, **"YOU'RE ONE TO THE RIDE THE RIVER WITH TIM."** Opened the driver's door, hopped down, jogged over to the helicopter, and jumped on board without hesitation. When

Fry's butt hit that seat, he left those **_"war nerves"_** behind, **_"igniting"_** an immense self-confidence that the pilots could *"trUst"* to guide them into the Indian Flats campsite.

Dr. Jack McMahon was an internal surgeon. Dr. C. Rollins Hanlon was a cardiac surgeon, and Dr. Peg Hanlon was a pediatrician. Thus, none of the three surgeons present at Indian Flats had ever performed burr hole surgery in their professional careers.

In 1973, burr hole surgery, also known as trepanation, was performed to relieve pressure from conditions resulting from blunt force trauma cranial injuries. The procedure involved *"drilling"* a small hole in the skull to access the brain and drain excess fluid or blood, thus relieving the life-threatening pressure building in the brain area.

Tools: The surgeon used a hand-held drill and a trephine, a circular saw-like instrument, to create the burr hole. *(Cain Kennedy, 2024, Shuntool.com)*

Procedure: The drill was applied with steady pressure to create a precise opening, allowing for controlled access to the brain. *(Wikipedia.org)*

Purpose: The burr hole was used to relieve pressure and facilitate the removal of blood or other materials from the brain. *(webbmd.com, hopkinsmedicine.com)*

Dr. Jack McMahon and Dr. C. Rollins Hanlon did not have a hand-held drill or the trephine circular saw listed above to drill the necessary burr hole in Tommy's skull. The small emergency medical kit Dr. Jack McMahon packed in his saddle bags contained sterilization fluid, local anesthesia, a couple of injection needles, and different variations of gauze, bandages, and wraps you would find in most common day first aid kits.

Before Dr. Jack McMahon had gone up on the ridge to help the children with the *"signal fire"* construction, Dr. C. Rollins Hanlon and himself designated the *"**tools**"* they would use to perform the burr hole field surgery on Tommy. A Swiss Army knife Dr. McMahon always carried in his pocket, and a pair of hemostat forceps that were attached to his fly jacket were the *"**chosen**"* drill and trephine circular saw burr hole tool replacements.

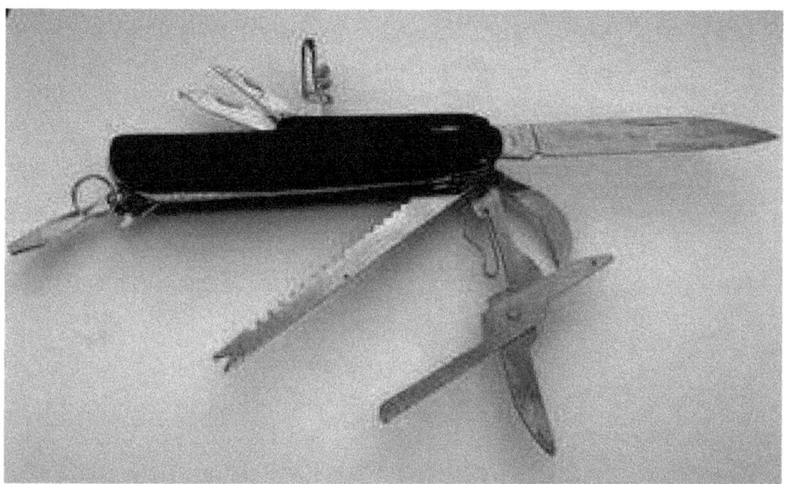

Photo of the **<u>"Actual"</u>** Swiss Army knife used in the burr hole surgery by Dr. Jack McMahon and Dr. C. Rollins Hanlon on Tommy McMahon, August 16, 1973, at the Indian Flats campsite.

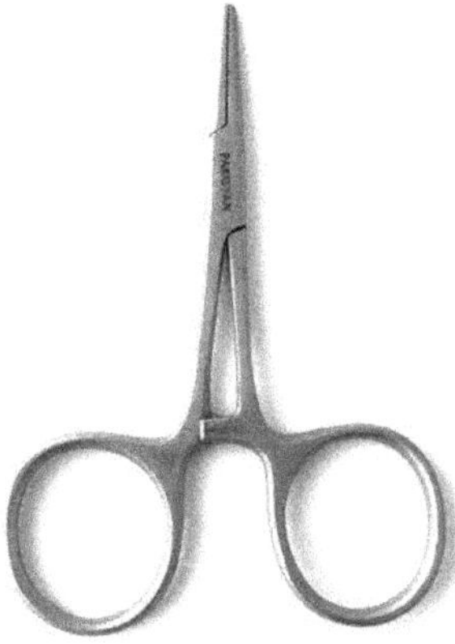

Internet photo of a **<u>"similar"</u>** Hemostat Forceps tool used in the burr hole surgery.

Dr. Jack McMahon took Tommy from Joanie's trembling hands and headed back to the "pack box" table Dr. C. Rollins Hanlon had **"prepared"** for the field surgery.

At approximately 10:30 PM, Dr. McMahon gently placed the boy on the "plywood operating table" between the towels, sterilization supplies, a bottle of anesthesia, and designated surgical tools. He then went to the campfire and "scrubbed" his hands in preparation for surgery.

It had been "agreed" upon by Dr. Jack McMahon and Dr. C. Rollins Hanlon that Dr. McMahon would perform the burr hole surgery on his son Tommy, and Dr. Hanlon would provide his expertise in a "verbal role" only.

The **"trUsted"** surgeon, Dr. Jack McMahon, returned to the operating table, leaving Tommy's father behind.

Jack flashed his flashlight in Tommy's unconscious eyes. His right eye had dilation in his right pupil, and there was no reaction to the light. Both of the child's eyes had developed rigidity at the "concerning" level, and his breath rate was alternating between the "rapid" and "apnea" levels within the Cheyne-Stokes respiration diagnosis Dr. Hanlon had delivered up on the landing site ridge.

"Jack, go around to the other side of the table with that lantern to provide a wider angle for the light to shine onto his head and give Tommy some stability with your other hand on his shoulder area." Dr. McMahon instructed Jack Jr.

"Jack, hand me your flashlight. I'll provide direct light from this side of the table for you," Dr. Hanlon said.

Dr. McMahon cleaned and sterilized the right side of Tommy's skull behind his right ear at the red and swollen blunt force injury site. This site is where the subsequent burr hole surgery would take place.

He applied some local anesthetic to the area using one of the needles from the emergency kit.

Dr. McMahon then went to work on the time-consuming process of "shaving" the boy's hair from the surgery site with the blade of the Swiss Army knife. Once the hair was shaved from the injured area, the surgeon once again cleaned and sterilized the injured area.

Dr. McMahon then began the burr hole procedure using the Swiss Army knife tools and hemostat forceps to slowly **"chip"** a hole in Tommy's skull to access the dura mater, which is the outermost layer of the meninges that protects the brain.

Upon reaching the dura mater layer, a couple of things stood out to the two surgeons.

"I see what I believe to be a small subgaleal clot there to the right next to those bone fragments, Jack," Dr. C. Rollins Hanlon pointed out.

"I see that also, and there is a fracture line present here," Dr. Jack McMahon said, using the narrow tip of the needle he used to deliver the anesthesia to point out the visible fracture.

"I do not believe you are through the skull enough, Jack. Keep chipping away those bone fragments a bit more to get to that clot to release the fluid," Dr. Hanlon instructed Dr. McMahon.

"His current breath rate has me extremely concerned," Dr. Jack McMahon stated as he slowly chipped away at the bone fragments in an attempt to complete the burr hole to get access to the clotted area.

"I agree the rate is elevating, yet getting that clotted blood drained will improve his condition. Need to be slow and steady in that area, Jack, due to the fracture. We do not want to enlarge that break line." Dr. Hanlon calmly guided his former med student.

Tommy's rapid breathing had sixteen-year-old Jack Jr. visibly upset. The tears slowly streaming down his cheeks had no effect on the *"consistently stable light"* he was providing the two surgeons, and the *"hidden strength"* his hand was providing on his brother's shoulders.

Dr. Jack McMahon eventually chipped away the bone fragments to the point where he could get to the small clot. Dr. McMahon was able to get a few cc's of clotted blood pressed out through the *"make-shift"* burr hole he had created.

Suddenly Tommy took a deep, deep, deep breath in. After what seemed like an eternity to Jack Jr. and the two surgeons, the child exhaled all that air out with one big push that sounded like timber falling in the forest around them.

Dr. Peg Hanlon, who was making her way up to check on Tommy for Joanie, heard the exhale and bolted to the camp table.

"What was that?" she asked in concern. **ZERO** response from either surgeon.

Dead silence overcame every inch of the Indian Flats campsite for the next five minutes, as Dr. Jack McMahon, Dr. C. Rollins Hanlon, Dr. Peg Hanlon, and Jack McMahon Jr. listened with *"relief"* as Tommy's breathing slowly returned to a ***"normal"*** level.

"There is a little more clotted blood there, Jack," Dr. C. Rollins Hanlon pointed out.

"His brain pulsation is improving," Dr. Jack McMahon observed through the burr hole area as he finished removing the last couple of cc's of the dark clotted blood with the hemostat forceps.

"Agree 100% Jack. We need to pack that wound with sterile gauze," Dr. Hanlon stated as he handed it to the surgeon in exchange for the hemostat forceps.

The two surgeons finished packing the burr hole area with gauze to prevent Tommy from bleeding out. By 12:45 A.M., the field surgery had been completed.

Dr. Peg Hanlon relayed the news of Tommy's stabilization to Joanie McMahon in the tent. Within thirty seconds, Joanie was on her way up to the camp table.

Jack McMahon Sr. met her halfway, silently holding her in his arms for comfort.

"I will hold up my end of that **PROMISE** made in the tent, yet we must not move him love," Jack whispered in her ear. Joanie nodded in acknowledgement as she gently kissed Jack on the cheek and made her way up to the camp table.

Joanie clasped both of Tommy's hands in hers. The child needed to remain "*immobile*" on that table, yet she "*yearned and prayed*" for the moment he would be back in her arms as **promised.**

"Jack, I need you to go up on that ridge and check on the "*signal fire*" for me. Be sure they have gathered enough wood for the possible three-hour burn we will need until daybreak. Once enough wood is gathered, I need the five of you to "*space*" out along the bottom of that open ridge line and walk slowly to the top "*clearing*" it of any downed timber that might hinder the chopper's landing. Take the sandwiches and fruit that Peg has prepared for them, also please." Jack Sr. instructed.

Jack Sr. then put his hands directly on Jack Jr's shoulders and looked him directly in the eyes, adding, "I understand how hard that was, for you to watch Tommy go through. You were strong, Son. Yet I am going to ask you to do something that may require even more strength. Jack, we need to keep what happened down here on that camp table between us until we can safely get Tommy out of here."

"I understand Dad. *"trUst"* me that fire will be lit at 3:00 A.M." Jack Jr. replied to his father in confidence.

CHAPTER 11:
THE RESCUE

At 1:45 A.M., it hit Dr. Jack McMahon that he had forgotten to secure a method for **_"transporting"_** the immobilized Tommy up to the landing site.

Plenty of time, no worries, he needed to secure one of the horses that were pasturing on the other side of the river.

A sense of **_"panic"_** crept into his mind as he listened into the night air. NO LOCATION BELLS COULD BE HEARD ON THE OTHER SIDE OF THE WEST FORK OF THE SUN RIVER!

Dr. McMahon hustled down to the tack area and discovered that Jack Jr. and Joe had _"innocently"_ forgotten to attach the _"location bells"_ onto any of the horses. Doc grabbed a halter and one of the location bells and headed back up to the camp table, where Tommy still lay unconscious with Joanie and both of the Hanlon doctors.

"Rollo, I need to get across the river and grab one of the horses to transport Tommy up to the helicopter when it arrives. I need you to stay here with Tommy. In an emergency, grab this bell and give it a good, hard ring. I will hear it and return to camp. Do not leave the campsite for any reason," Dr. Jack McMahon instructed.

"Will not leave his side Jack," Dr. Hanlon said, reassuring his father that Tommy was in "trUsted" hands.

Dr. McMahon pointed his flashlight toward the river and made his way down to its edge. He quickly waded across the dark, chilly waters of the West Fork of the Sun River. Doc did not use Joe's *"trick"* of shaking a canvas bucket full of pellets for two reasons:

1. All of the canvas buckets were filled with water, sitting up on the ridge of the landing site, ready to extinguish the "*signal fire.*"
2. Jack Sr. did NOT know the trick even existed – he rarely wrangled the stock at home or in The Bob due to the fact that two or three of his ten children or two of the wranglers were assigned that duty.

Dr. McMahon's flashlight found a game trail with *"plenty"* of horse tracks on it. He followed that trail through timbered areas that would occasionally open into small backcountry meadows. No horses and dead silence. His mental clock was telling him he was eating up too much precious time, and his stomach went into a twisted panic of nerves.

Doc continued following the horse-hooved game trail. Back up the trail where he had just come from, he heard a branch break. Dr. McMahon realized one of the mules or horses was now heading in his direction. Anxiously, he made his way back in the direction he came. Within one minute, he walked right into the gentle giant Chief.

Dr. McMahon threw the halter on Chief and wrapped the lead rope around his neck to form a circular reining system. Using his flashlight to find a tree stump he could use as a step ladder, he was quickly on the back of the appaloosa gelding heading back to the Indian Flats campsite.

During the fifteen-minute ride back to camp, Dr. McMahon began to plan the transport of Tommy to the helicopter in his mind. Chief, the legendary rodeo bucking horse, would **NOT** tolerate a riding saddle with any form of human passenger, yet would he tolerate a *"packsaddle"* loaded with an injured Tommy who must remain *"immobile"*?

At 3:00 A.M. on the button, Missy, Martha, Mary, Joe, and Jack Jr. lit the "signal fire" as instructed by Dr. McMahon. Little did they know Dick Fryhover was simultaneously hopping into a helicopter, lifting off from a grassy airstrip in Augusta.

"Dick and Bob, I won't need any guidance until we pass over that Benchmark Trailhead. Once we fly over, I will let you both know when I need some guidance. Until then, hold onto your ass, we have one hell of a headwind to break through for the next forty-five minutes in order to get to that campsite." Pilot Capt. Buck Buchanan radioed the flight plan into Dick Fryhover and District Ranger Bob Duncan's headsets as they made their way from Augusta to Benchmark.

"Roger that, Captain," Fry and Bob acknowledged.

The HH-43 "Huskie" Air Force rescue chopper pushed through the head winds and soon Capt. Buck Buchanan was reaching out to Dick Fryhover over the headset.

"About over the top of that trailhead at Benchmark now, Dick. It looks like four river valleys split off up here. Which one do I start up into?" Capt. Buck Buchanan calmly asked.

"The second one from the left, Captain," Fry instructed the pilot as Bob Duncan nodded his head in agreement.

"Roger that," Capt. Buchanan replied and guided the HH-43 "Huskie" up the valley.

Three minutes later, Capt. Buchanan came back on the headset, "Dick, this valley looks like it splits up here. Which way, left or right, do you want me to take this bird?"

"Left Captain. The signal fire will be up this valley on your left in about ten miles," Dick responded as Sun River District Ranger Duncan again nodded in agreement.

"What am I heading into from a landing site perspective, Dick?" Capt. Buck Buchanan inquired as he pushed the chopper through the blasting headwind.

"It is an open meadowed ridge line about three to four hundred yards from the campsite. Plenty of room for the chopper, yet there is some "*grade*" to that slope as you will see when you throw your under lights onto it," Fry replied, trying not to hold back any pertinent detail.

"I heard the plan you laid out with the dispatcher to get the fire out before we touch down, yet is there a plan in place to get the patient up to the landing site?" Copilot Lt. James M. McKee questioned Fry.

"If not, we may need to drop you to retrieve the patient and come back a second time to get him. Don't know if I can hold this bird on that slope if the wind is blowing like this on that steep ridge." Pilot Capt. Buck Buchanan added into the headset.

"Yes, a transport plan from the campsite to the landing site is in place. Jack McMahon will have Tommy there," Dick Fryhover reassured the two pilots.

Dr. Jack McMahon heard the faint sound of a chopper fighting its way up the West Fork of the Sun River Valley.

"Rollo, Peg, Joanie, do you hear that?" Dr. McMahon anxiously inquired as he began to make his way to retrieve Chief for transport.

"Is that a helicopter?" Dr. Peg Hanlon shot back.

"That is definitely the sound of chopper rotors," Dr. C. Rollins Hanlon responded.

Up on the ridge, the noise of the signal fire burning was still drowning out the sound of the approaching helicopter.

Dr. C. Rollins Hanlon and Dr. Jack McMahon picked up the small *"makeshift plywood emergency backboard"* that Tommy was securely tied down to, rendering him *"immobile"* for transport. Dr. Peg Hanlon held the lead rope of Chief while the two men slowly raised the child over the Appaloosa's hind quarters, slowly walking the backboard up to the D-rings of the Decker Packsaddle. Dr. Jack McMahon threw a rope over to Dr. C. Rollins Hanlon, and the surgeons secured Tommy to the packsaddle.

"There's the signal fire, good men," Capt. Buck Buchanan declared over the headsets.

As the chopper passed over the *"signal fire"* Missy, Mary, Martha, Joe, and Jack Jr. began dousing the fire with the water that had been hauled up from the Indian Flats campsite.

"You feel that, James? The wind just went dead," Capt. Buck Buchanan asked his copilot.

"Let's pray it stays that way for the next fifteen minutes Buck," Lt. James M. McKee replied as Capt. Buck Buchanan flipped the under lights of the helicopter on and turned the bird back in the direction of the identified landing site.

Dick Fryhover couldn't help but wonder if that massive limestone structure seven miles up that valley, known as the Chinese Wall, was by ***"divine intervention"***, knocking that wind down for them?

Dr. Jack McMahon was a good fifty yards down the trail by now, heading in the direction of the landing site, leading Chief with Tommy securely stabilized on the packsaddle. The noise and ground wind the chopper created while turning around had NO EFFECT on the bucking horse's relaxed temperament.

Captain Buck Buchanan circled the landing site a couple of times to allow the under lights to give him a solid picture of what he was heading into. The grade of the ridge was exactly what Dick Fryhover had described. Buck would have to be sure to touch the chopper down facing down the hill to secure the rescue.

This delay in landing also bought time for the children to get the *"signal fire"* out, and for Dr. Jack McMahon to close the distance between the campsite and the ridge.

Captain Buck Buchanan set that bird down on the bottom right edge of the steep ridge line and lowered the propulsion of the two main rotors, while keeping the back rotor propulsion up to provide stability to the aircraft.

Dick Fryhover swung the door open, hopped out, and looked through the wind-swept grass. Out of the left corner of his eye, he noticed a light steadily moving across the dark ridge line towards the chopper at a consistent pace.

As Dr. Jack McMahon came into view, Dick Fryhover could not believe his eyes and stated in bewilderment, **"He must be crazy. He chose Chief."**

Doc didn't even break stride, leading Chief all the way to that chopper's door. Dropped his halter rope as the main rotors spun slowly above the gelding, and with the help of Dick Fryhover, untied Tommy from the pack saddle and loaded his son into the helicopter.

Before Jack Sr. hopped into the chopper, he put his hand on Dick's shoulder, looked him in the eyes, and hollered, "You will **see** him again Dick."

"I'll hold you to that partner," Fry hollered back confidently, knowing that the surgeon's ***"word had always been their bond."***

Tim Gleason made it back to the corral area at the Benchmark Trailhead to find Gerado and Charley in good condition. Tim unsaddled the two quarter horses, brushed the froth that had developed from the sweat off their coats, watered them, and began to slowly feed them a mixture of oats and pellets. Horses that have *"been run"* hard for great distances must be slowly fed; allowing them to gorge quickly to satisfy their hunger needs can lead to serious issues.

The sound of helicopter rotors caught Gerado, Charley, and Tim's attention. The trio looked up to see the HH-43 "Huskie" Air Force rescue chopper pass over the corral area on its way to Deaconess Hospital in Great Falls.

Tim Gleason watched the red flashing lights of the helicopter disappear out of sight into the darkness. The *"known"* objective was to secure the evacuation helicopter = completed, yet his mind went to where that chopper was headed. Would the chopper get there in time? As Tim reached into the canvas bucket of pellets and fed a handful to Gerado, the **"gravity of that moment"** overtook the tough wrangler.

CHAPTER 12:
THE POSTCARD

Thomas Stephen McMahon, now known as *"Tom,"* graduated from Capital High School in Helena, Montana, on June 2, 1988. The next morning, he planned to leave the family ranch up Moose Creek and move into town to begin the next chapter of his life.

Joanie McMahon **HELD** Tom in her arms, as Jack Sr. had **PROMISED** she would **AGAIN**, then sent him on his way with two pieces of her legendary cinnamon toast.

As Tom opened up the driver's door of his pickup, he noticed a **postcard** with a photo of the Chinese Wall and an old red **Swiss Army knife** sitting on the seat. Picking up the postcard, he turned it over, and it simply said:

"tr<u>U</u>st"

I Know...

Pops

Why the letter "**U**" capitalized in the word "tr**U**st", one may ask? That "**U**" represents the most important person we must learn to tr**U**st = yo**U**rself. On the night of August 16, 1973, inner "tr**U**st" was brought to a **LEVEL** never seen before by all inhabitants of that Indian Flats campsite through their selfless actions, resulting in **LIFE** being ***"chipped"*** back into Tommy by that Swiss Army knife.

"A night of miracles," Tim Gleason called it during the phone conversation we recently had as I was researching the events of that 1973 evening in **"The Bob."**

As a father and the author of this real-life event, I cannot imagine **_"burring"_** a hole into my child's skull. The **_"paternal lifelong guilt"_** that could come from ending my child's life with a Swiss Army knife would be overwhelming.

Tom's father, Jack Sr., had always been his **_"I know"_** through those first eighteen years of his life. Somehow, someway, that man he affectionately called **_"Pops"_** always **"knew"** when something was awry inside him, and it was immediately fixed with a **_"Doc talk."_**

Tom pulled out of the driveway with his heart in his throat, full of **gratefulness** to Capt. Buck Buchanan, Lt. James M. McKee, Sun River District Ranger Bob Duncan, Dr. C. Rollins Hanlon, Dr. Peg Hanlon, Sarah Hanlon, Martha Hanlon, Mary Hanlon, Dr. Jack McMahon Sr., Joanie McMahon, Jack McMahon Jr., Joe McMahon, Missy McMahon, Toots McMahon, Mike McMahon, Tim McMahon, Oly McMahon, Tim Gleason, and Dick Fryhover.

As Tom reached the bottom cattle guard, he recognized a **_"white Chevy Suburban"_** pulling up the gravel road. Tom pulled over and rolled down his pickup window.

Dick Fryhover, **<u>SAW</u>** Tom, as Jack Sr. had **PROMISED** he would **<u>AGAIN</u>**, rolled down his window with a big smile on his face, and hollered, **_"How was graduation, Slick?"_**

... WORD HAD ALWAYS BEEN THEIR BOND ...

CHAPTER 13:
SHARED WITH YOU...

Attached a photo, newspaper articles, and hospital records I felt compelled to share with you as the reader...

Left to Right: *Dick Fryhover, Jack McMahon Sr., and their **"beloved"** granddaughter, Quincy McMahon, in 2006 at the University of Louisville vs. West Virginia football game at Papa John's Stadium in Louisville, Kentucky.*

Doctor performs field surgery to save son

GREAT FALLS, Mont. (AP) — A 4-year-old boy, on whom emergency head surgery was performed by his surgeon father, was flown from a Montana wilderness area by helicopter early today to a Great Falls hospital.

An Air Force spokesman said the boy, Thomas S. McMahon, son of Dr. and Mrs. John McMahon, Helena, fell from a horse about 6:30 p.m. Thursday while on a pack trip with his family and that of another surgeon, Dr. C. Rawlins Hanlon.

To save the boy, who struck his head in the fall, the two surgeons performed a field operation as their guide and outfitter, Dick Fryhover, and a 17-year-old assistant, Tim Gleason, rode horseback through the rugged area 10 miles in the dark to the Benchmark Ranger Station.

Unable to get through to authorities on the ranger's radiotelephone, Fryhover drove to the town of Augusta to call for help and the Air Force helicopter was dispatched from Malmstrom Air Force Base in Great Falls about 2:45 a.m.

The helicopter and crew — Capt. Buck Buchanan and Lt. James McGee — stopped at Augusta to pick up the Sun River District ranger, Bob Duncan, who guided the craft to the accident scene.

Later, in a Great Falls hospital, the boy's condition was listed as critical.

McMahon boy released

GREAT FALLS (AP) — A 4-year-old Helena boy who underwent emergency surgery by flashlight in the Bob Marshall Wilderness earlier this month has been released from a Great Falls hospital.

Thomas S. McMahon, son of Dr. and Mrs. John W. McMahon, underwent surgery Aug. 16 after receiving head injuries from a fall off a horse.

His father and Dr. C Rawlins Hanlon, who are both surgeons, performed emergency head surgery on the boy to relieve pressure from the brain. The boy was taken in a Air Force helicopter to a Great Falls hospital where is was orginally listed in critical condition.

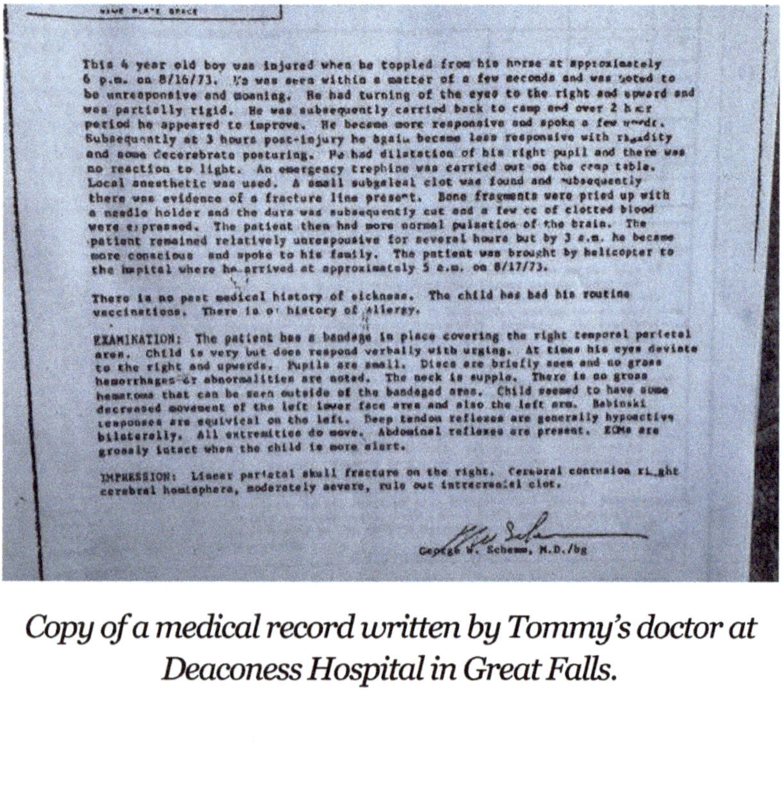

This 4 year old boy was injured when he toppled from his horse at approximately 6 p.m. on 8/16/73. He was seen within a matter of a few seconds and was noted to be unresponsive and moaning. He had turning of the eyes to the right and upward and was partially rigid. He was subsequently carried back to camp and over 2 hour period he appeared to improve. He became more responsive and spoke a few words. Subsequently at 3 hours post-injury he again became less responsive with rigidity and some decerebrate posturing. He had dilatation of his right pupil and there was no reaction to light. An emergency trephine was carried out on the camp table. Local anesthetic was used. A small subgaleal clot was found and subsequently there was evidence of a fracture line present. Bone fragments were pried up with a needle holder and the dura was subsequently cut and a few cc of clotted blood were expressed. The patient then had more normal pulsation of the brain. The patient remained relatively unresponsive for several hours but by 3 a.m. he became more conscious and spoke to his family. The patient was brought by helicopter to the hospital where he arrived at approximately 5 a.m. on 8/17/73.

There is no past medical history of sickness. The child has had his routine vaccinations. There is no history of allergy.

EXAMINATION: The patient has a bandage in place covering the right temporal parietal area. Child is very but does respond verbally with urging. At times his eyes deviate to the right and upwards. Pupils are small. Discs are briefly seen and no gross hemorrhages or abnormalities are noted. The neck is supple. There is no gross hematoma that can be seen outside of the bandaged area. Child seemed to have some decreased movement of the left lower face area and also the left arm. Babinski responses are equivical on the left. Deep tendon reflexes are generally hypoactive bilaterally. All extremities do move. Abdominal reflexes are present. EOMs are grossly intact when the child is more alert.

IMPRESSION: Linear parietal skull fracture on the right. Cerebral contusion right cerebral hemisphere, moderately severe, rule out intracranial clot.

George W. Schemm, M.D./bg

Copy of a medical record written by Tommy's doctor at
Deaconess Hospital in Great Falls.

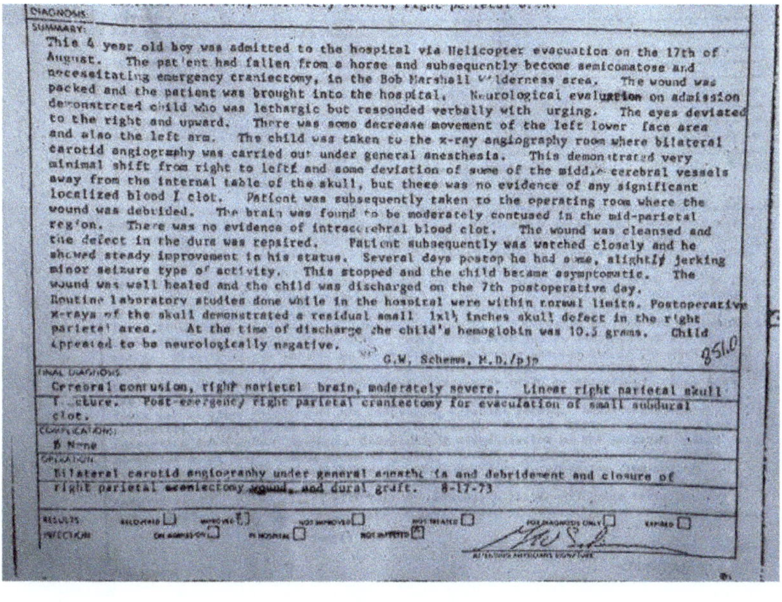

DIAGNOSIS:

SUMMARY:

This 4 year old boy was admitted to the hospital via Helicopter evacuation on the 17th of August. The patient had fallen from a horse and subsequently become semicomatose and necessitating emergency craniectomy, in the Bob Marshall Wilderness area. The wound was packed and the patient was brought into the hospital. Neurological evaluation on admission demonstrated child who was lethargic but responded verbally with urging. The eyes deviated to the right and upward. There was some decrease movement of the left lower face area and also the left arm. The child was taken to the x-ray angiography room where bilateral carotid angiography was carried out under general anesthesia. This demonstrated very minimal shift from right to left and some deviation of some of the middle cerebral vessels away from the internal table of the skull, but there was no evidence of any significant localized blood I clot. Patient was subsequently taken to the operating room where the wound was debrided. The brain was found to be moderately contused in the mid-parietal region. There was no evidence of intracerebral blood clot. The wound was cleansed and the defect in the dura was repaired. Patient subsequently was watched closely and he showed steady improvement in his status. Several days postop he had some, slightly jerking minor seizure type of activity. This stopped and the child became asymptomatic. The wound was well healed and the child was discharged on the 7th postoperative day. Routine laboratory studies done while in the hospital were within normal limits. Postoperative x-rays of the skull demonstrated a residual small 1x1½ inches skull defect in the right parietal area. At the time of discharge the child's hemoglobin was 10.5 grams. Child appeared to be neurologically negative.

G.W. Schems, M.D./pjp

851.0

FINAL DIAGNOSIS

Cerebral contusion, right parietal brain, moderately severe. Linear right parietal skull fracture. Post-emergency right parietal craniectomy for evacuation of small subdural clot.

COMPLICATIONS

B None

OPERATION

Bilateral carotid angiography under general anesthesia and debridement and closure of right parietal craniectomy wound, and dural graft. 8-17-73

RESULTS   RECOVERED ☐   IMPROVED ☒   NOT IMPROVED ☐   NOT TREATED ☐   FOR DIAGNOSIS ONLY ☐   EXPIRED ☐
INFECTION: ON ADMISSION ☐   IN HOSPITAL ☐   NOT INFECTED ☒

ATTENDING PHYSICIAN'S SIGNATURE

Copy of a medical record written by Tommy's doctor at Deaconess Hospital in Great Falls.

Anesthetic Used: _______________________   Started: _______ 0001 _______ Ended: _______ 1020 _______
Operation Started: _______ 110 ___ 0000 _______________   Ended: _______________ 1011 _______________
Immediate Postoperative Condition, etc.: ____

Dictate Separately   Findings: (Including the Condition of all organs examined. Note if not examined.)
                      What Was Done: (Including Incision, Ligatures, Sutures, Drainage and Closure.)

The patient was anesthetized and the neck extended in the aniography room. #20 longdwell
needles were put in place and injections of approximately 6 cc of 60% Conray were made
on both sides in lateral and AP positions. The x-rays were essentially negative with
the exception of some elevation of the right middle cerebral vessels. A linear parietal
skull fracture was apparent on the right side. The patient was then taken to the
operating room where the entire head was prepped and subsequently the right side of the
head prepped and draped as sterile field. On removing the packing from the wound the
defect in the skull was visualized as well as the underlying pulsating brain tissue.
There is evidence of some superficial laceration of the cortical surface and considerable
contusion to the surface of the brain. Retractors were put in place to retract the
scalp. Periosteum was incised so as to allow complete visualization of the bone defect
which was approximately 2 cm in length by 1.5 cm in width. Subsequently it was necessary
to enlarge the bony opening back to where intact dura could be visualized. This dura
was trimmed of macerated lacerated edges. Dural retraction sutures were put in place.
There was no gross bleeding of the underlying cerebral cortex. There was a small
collection of xanthochromic subdural hydroma fluid. This was readily evacuated upon
depressing the cortical surface. Subsequently visualization of the parietal cortex
posterior to the bony opening revealed further contusion of the brain surface but no
gross laceration and no active bleeding. A ventricular catheter was then passed
approximately 4 cm slightly posteriorly and deeply into the parietal lobe area without
encountering a   gross cystic clot cavity. The brain tissue was quite soft, however.
Subsequently closure was carried out. A small piece of temporalis muscle fascia was

                              (over)
                                                        _______________________ M.D.
                                                              SURGEON
                                                        OPERATION # 19-5838

Tommy's Deaconess Hospital operation record from the morning of his admittance, August 17, 1973, upon arrival by helicopter from the Indian Flats campsite.

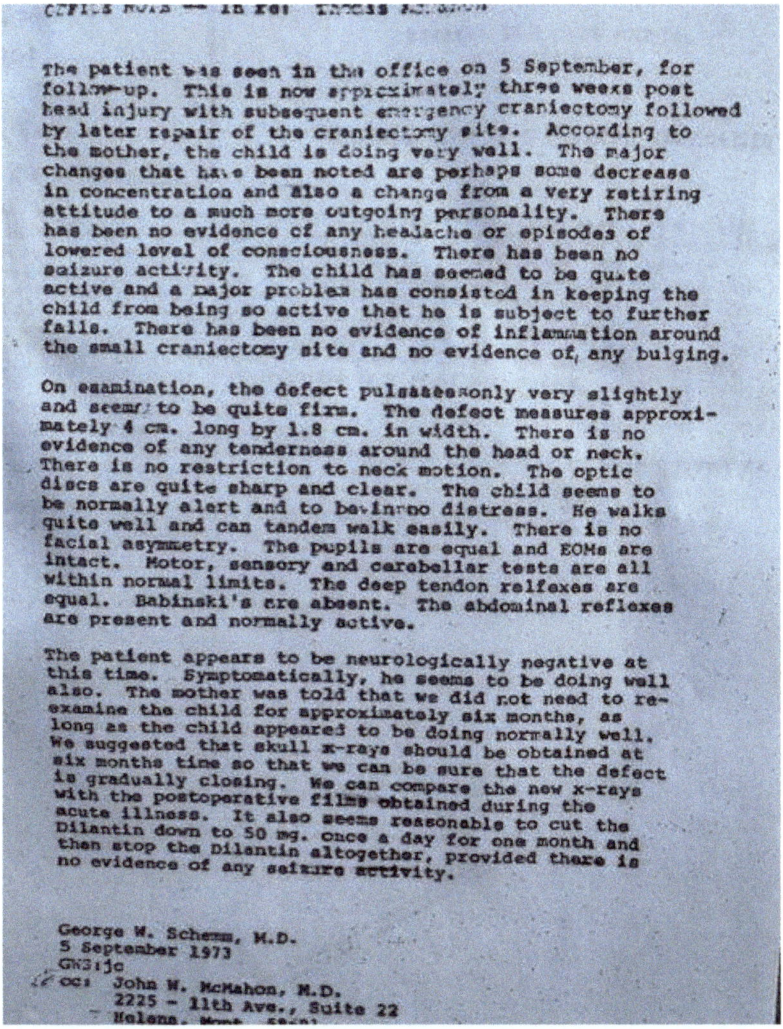

OFFICE NOTE -- in re: [illegible]

The patient was seen in the office on 5 September, for
follow-up. This is now approximately three weeks post
head injury with subsequent emergency craniectomy followed
by later repair of the craniectomy site. According to
the mother, the child is doing very well. The major
changes that have been noted are perhaps some decrease
in concentration and also a change from a very retiring
attitude to a much more outgoing personality. There
has been no evidence of any headache or episodes of
lowered level of consciousness. There has been no
seizure activity. The child has seemed to be quite
active and a major problem has consisted in keeping the
child from being so active that he is subject to further
falls. There has been no evidence of inflammation around
the small craniectomy site and no evidence of any bulging.

On examination, the defect pulsates only very slightly
and seems to be quite firm. The defect measures approximately 4 cm. long by 1.8 cm. in width. There is no
evidence of any tenderness around the head or neck.
There is no restriction to neck motion. The optic
discs are quite sharp and clear. The child seems to
be normally alert and to be in no distress. He walks
quite well and can tandem walk easily. There is no
facial asymmetry. The pupils are equal and EOMs are
intact. Motor, sensory and cerebellar tests are all
within normal limits. The deep tendon reflexes are
equal. Babinski's are absent. The abdominal reflexes
are present and normally active.

The patient appears to be neurologically negative at
this time. Symptomatically, he seems to be doing well
also. The mother was told that we did not need to re-
examine the child for approximately six months, as
long as the child appeared to be doing normally well.
We suggested that skull x-rays should be obtained at
six months time so that we can be sure that the defect
is gradually closing. We can compare the new x-rays
with the postoperative films obtained during the
acute illness. It also seems reasonable to cut the
Dilantin down to 50 mg. once a day for one month and
then stop the Dilantin altogether, provided there is
no evidence of any seizure activity.

George W. Schemm, M.D.
5 September 1973
GWS:jc
cc: John W. McMahon, M.D.
     2225 - 11th Ave., Suite 22
     Helena, Mont. 59601

*Follow-up visit with Tommy's doctor in Great Falls,
Montana, 9/5/1973.*

Mc Mahon, Thomas S.

Room: 621-2

Case #: 240229

Admitted 3/28/74

NAME PLATE SPACE

MONTANA DEACONESS HOSPITAL
Great Falls, Montana

PERSONAL HISTORY & PHYSICAL EXAMINATION

This 4 year old boy was admitted to the hospital for cranioplasty repair of a right parietal skull defect. The patient had an entry to the right side of the head associated with skull fracture and cerebral contusion on 8/17/73. The patient had signs of neurological deterioration acutely and underwent emergency operation on the same day. Patient was then brought to the hospital where bilateral carotid angiography was done followed by debridement and closure of the craniectomy wound. Patient has done very well since that time and is on no medications. He has had no evidence of any intra-cranial problems and no seizure activity. The skull defect has persisted, however, and x-rays demonstrated there is no decrease in size of this defect.

EXAMINATION:
    HEART, LUNGS & ABDOMEN: Unremarkable.
    NEUROLOGICAL: Is also grossly intact. There is a pulsating type skull defect in the right mid parietal area.

INITIAL IMPRESSION: Residual skull defect secondary to head injury and craniectomy carried out 8 months ago.

Tommy had to go back to Deaconess Hospital in Great Falls, Montana, eight months after his initial discharge, on March 28, 1974. The burr hole area in his skull was not producing regrowth over the opening appropriately, = skull defect described above.

ADMITTING
DIAGNOSIS: skull defect, right parietal area

SUMMARY
        This 4 year old boy was readmitted to the hospital for repair of a skull defect
which was secondary to an emergency craniectomy carried out for possible intracranial
clot in August 1973. The patient had done very well and was neurologically negative
but had continued to have a moderate sized skull defect approximately 2X3cm in
dimensions which had failed to show any signs of closure over the past 8 months.
This was in a young active boy and it was felt important to repair the defect to
prevent the possibly injury to the brain in this area. Neurological examination
was negative. The pulsating type skull defect was noted in the right mid parietal
area. Following initial evaluation operation was carried out on 3-29-74 and an
acrylic cranioplasty was carried out without incident and the patient tolerated
the procedure well and the wound appeared to be healing with problems. He was
subsequently discharged on the 5th postoperative day with the sutures to be
removed and the wound followed by his father on an outpatient basis.

FINAL DIAGNOSIS
        skull defect, right mid parietal skull

COMPLICATIONS
        none

PROCEDURES
        acrylic cranioplasty for parietal skull defect. 3-29-74

March 29, 1974, acrylic cranioplasty surgery, doctor's notes. Surgeons fixed Tommy's skull defect = hole, by inserting an acrylic plate in his head that is with him to this day.